The New East Design and Style in Asia

MICHAEL FREEMAN

RIZZOLI
NEW YORK

The New Orient 16

Space 62

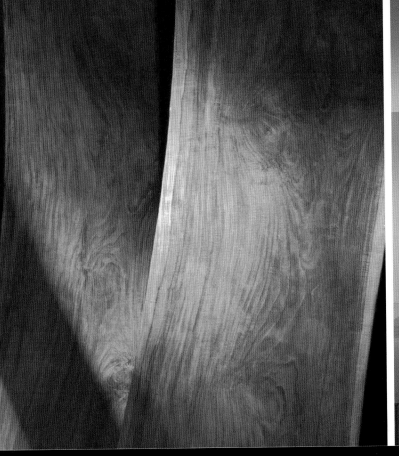

Materials 146

Essence 210

Handmade *washi* paper covers bamboo poles at An Restaurant in Tokyo's Daikanyama, pressing them into the wall (*page 1*).

In the view from a modern version of a traditional Japanese room, the small garden outside can be transformed from a *karezansui* (Zen drystone garden) into a pond. Here both are shown in a combined image (*title pages*).

On the busy concourse of Shinagawa station in Tokyo, a mendicant Zen monk rings a small bell as he waits for alms from commuters who are usually too pressed for time to notice (*opposite*).

Seen from the mouth of the Suzhou river as it enters the Huangpu at Shanghai, the opposite bank of Pudong has been transformed in only a few years from farmland into a high-rise extension of the metropolis (*pages 8–9*).

A newly pedestrianized part of the fashionable Ginza district of Tokyo, which continues to maintain its reputation for exclusive and expensive shopping and entertainment (*pages 10–11*).

A sushi chef in a new, minimally designed restaurant in Tokyo (*pages 12–13*).

First published in the United States of America in 2007 by
Rizzoli International Publications, Inc.
300 Park Avenue South, New York, NY 10010
www.rizzoliusa.com

First published in the United Kingdom in 2006 by
Thames & Hudson Ltd
181A High Holborn, London WC1V 7QX

Text and photography © 2006 Michael Freeman
Digital post-production: Yukako Shibata

ISBN-10: 0-8478-2914-6
ISBN-13: 978-0-8478-2914-9

Library of Congress Control Number: 2006929642

2007 2008 2009 2010 / 10 9 8 7 6 5 4 3 2 1

Printed and bound in China

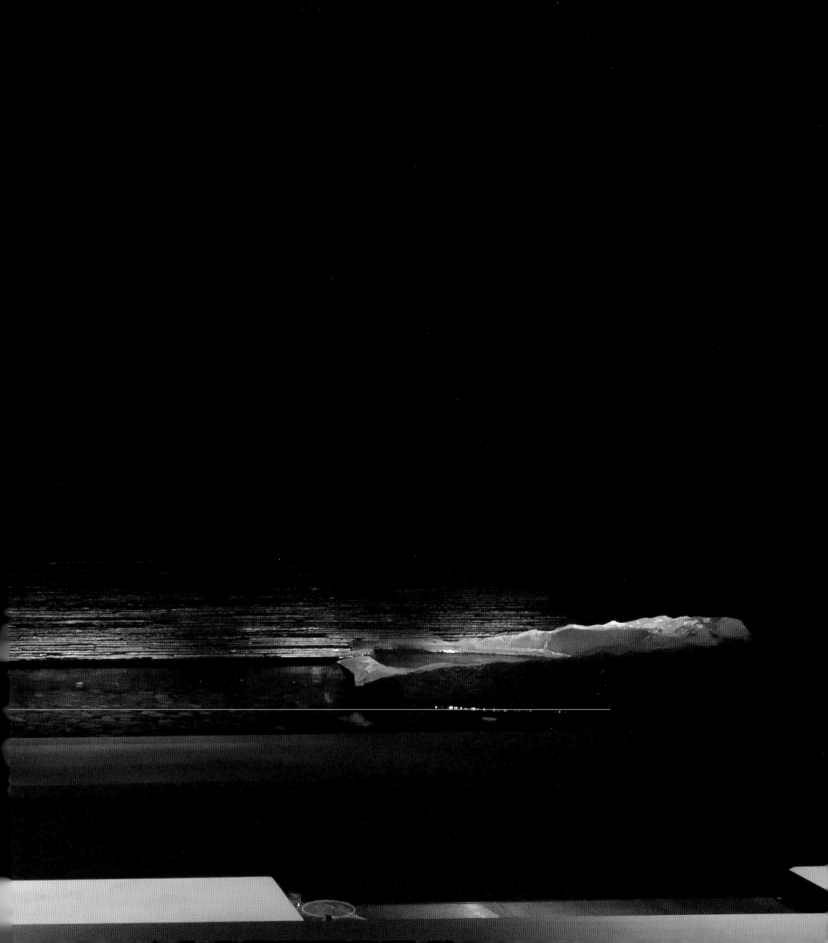

{introduction}

This book follows, after sixteen years, the original *In The Oriental Style*. Much has changed since then, changes which justify a fresh look at what is happening in modern Asian architecture and design, and at our perceptions of it. One phenomenon of that period that was to set off a train of design consequences was the pricking of Japan's economic bubble. Until then, the undisputed engine of Asian economic development had been booming since the mid-1960s. A number of other economies had followed this upwards trend, and they too were halted — for a while. But the effect of this on design and architecture was in the long run salutary rather than damaging. Another, more recent phenomenon, which promises to overshadow all others, is of course the change in the economy and self-confidence of China.

Every Asian country has undergone development in architecture and design during the past few decades, though at different speeds and not necessarily in the same ways. Yet all have been strongly influenced by an innate traditionalism that pervaded most Oriental societies until well into the twentieth century, despite some determined efforts to westernize, as during the Meiji era in Japan and the roughly concurrent reign of King Chulalongkorn in Thailand, and despite huge political upheavals, as the revolution in China. Historically, this traditionalism has had much to do with the philosophical conservatism of Confucianism and Buddhism; in designing dwellings this has often been translated into a satisfaction that once a design has been reached that works for the society and economy, there is little need to change it. The negative aspects of this are all too obvious, but the benefits are that traditional forms have a great deal to teach us, even when the exact reasons for their existence have long since disappeared.

In architecture and design, Japan had the post-war advantage of an economic headstart, and has until now led the way in imagination and sophistication. Its development has followed an almost decade-by-decade sequence. In the immediate post-war years, modernism was seen as the answer to reconstruction, not least because of its inherent simplicity, but incorporated in this were strange juxtapositions with traditional forms. By the 1960s, new economic optimism gave rise to the Metabolist movement, with its extravagant, monumental, industrial technology. During the 1970s, as the economy was really developing, reaction to this and the earlier modernist approach came in different forms, including an often trite and bizarre form of postmodernism and other style movements, such as Tadao Ando's concrete minimalism. The 1980s were the bubble years of unbridled experimentation, unlimited budgets, and a general excess all round, but also of innovative architecture. Finally, with the end of the bubble there has been a re-evaluation of Japan's long architectural and design tradition, and a search for an

An open wall of travertine slabs (*opposite left*) reflected in the glass wall of a bathroom at the Lotus House (*page 64*).

The bedroom of Art Space N (*opposite right*) (*page 256*).

A small, deep courtyard garden (*left*) at basement level in a house in Tokyo's Bunkyoku (*page 232*).

architecture better in tune with new lifestyles in an increasingly information-based economy.

This half-century of often contradictory progress was denied to Japan's much larger neighbour, but China's turn has now come with its rapid transformation into a market-led economy. With the lessons of the evolution of other countries' architectural and design styles before it, but with other needs, China's progress on these fronts will undoubtedly be different. Nevertheless, as Japanese architect Kengo Kuma, who has worked in both countries, says, 'I believe that every country and every city has its own construction age, much like every person has his or her adolescence. During this age, people dedicate themselves to large-scale construction projects that set the form of the city or country for years to come ... It is clear to me that modern China is coming into her adolescence.'

Other countries that have reached the stage of producing interesting contemporary designs for living include Korea, Taiwan, Thailand, Singapore and Malaysia, all with different dynamics. Yet other countries have not yet reached 'critical mass' in design development — a stage that needs both a sizable body of architects and interior designers to have emerged, and a reasonable number of potential clients who are willing to experiment with their own homes and other premises, and who can afford the investment. The island of Bali, from which several examples in this book are drawn, is a special case — a society that has so far successfully absorbed tourism and a large expatriate community, while still maintaining a very traditional and conservative lifestyle for most of its indigenous population.

This book is by no means a complete encyclopedia of modern architecture and design in Asia, and some countries have had to be omitted. The reason for this is that too much is happening too rapidly over a huge area for such completeness to be even worth considering. It seemed more worthwhile to develop the theme of how a new generation of cutting-edge Asian architects and designers is analysing and planning for the new dynamics of living. This is happening in regions that are at once loaded with traditional precepts and forms, and at the same time undergoing the most rapid changes of anywhere in the global economy during the early twenty-first century.

The examples which follow represent the ideals of a number of thoughtful people and imaginative, questioning architects and designers, not afraid to re-interpret time-honoured styles in new materials of the various regions in new and exciting forms. I have chosen to highlight here what I consider to be the great traditional virtues of Oriental design: the manipulation and articulation of space; the ingenious use of materials; and the striving after the expression of what is essential in a structure or interior. This book is an attempt to examine the application of these concerns in the new, vibrant design of the Orient.

{1. The New Orient}

One of the themes running through this book is that, despite the economic and societal differences between the countries represented here, there has been a fundamental re-evaluation of traditional forms since the early 1990s. This does not imply re-adoption and pastiche — there is no general interest anywhere in taking up antique designs for new living spaces. In addition, there has been a realization that simply indulging in a hodge-podge of international styles and importing Western architecture wholesale is neither appropriate nor particularly interesting. Instead, there is increasingly a sense of the need to find architectural and design vocabularies that are appropriate to modern Asian lifestyles — particularly urban lifestyles — and which also draw on principles that have been found to work for generations. These include, for example, the Chinese courtyard house, as found in the *siheyuan* ('four-sided enclosed courtyard') in the *hutongs* that are the characteristic and traditional pattern of urban dwelling associated especially with Beijing. Another influential concept is the interpenetration of exterior and interior spaces, the flexible partition of space, as in the Japanese tradition of sliding screens and floor-level living (*tatami* culture) that extends to Thailand and much of southeast Asia.

Making this translation is by no means always straightforward, for despite the wealth of tradition on which to draw, there are the obvious dangers of mimicry and irrelevance, and sometimes cultural resistance. In Thailand, for example, the sanctity of religious and regal architecture must be respected. However, the pages that follow in this section of the book do reveal a world of dynamic exchange. A 'Thai' restaurant in Tokyo is not just a reconstruction of an establishment in Bangkok or Chiang Mai, but an interpretation of the way the Japanese regard 'Thai-ness'. The buildings and artifacts of hard-line Communist China have been granted new roles in the market-led economy. And, most importantly, the cross-fertilization of tradition and the entirely contemporary, in material and content, is amply illustrated in this first evocation of contemporary architecture and design in the new Orient.

Art Deco stained-glass window (*opposite left*) in the Peace Hotel on the Bund, Shanghai (originally Sassoon House, built in 1929).

Fashion accessories shop Club 21 in the Erawan Bangkok shopping mall (*opposite right*).

Detail from a modern Korean restaurant, Zassou-ya (*below left*).

In a new subway station, Daimon, on Tokyo's Oedo line, architect Ken Yokogawa chose 'ink' as the theme (*below right*).

{Tsunami Restaurant, Bangkok} This Thai interpretation of a Japanese restaurant in Bangkok was handled by interior design group PIA, under its director Rujiraporn Wanglee. One of its central themes was derived from the all-important marine component in Japanese cuisine, and the name chosen was 'Tsunami' ('tidal wave'). Although the word became all too familiar after the 2004 tragedy in south-east Asia, the owners took the long view and retained it, though splitting it in two, *tsu* and *nami* to refer to the two different cuisines on offer — *izakaya*-style and *teppanyaki*. Nevertheless, one of the great successes in this design is the huge linking element that traverses most of the length of the underground space, a giant undulating wave that, while clearly inspired by a tsunami, also manages to evoke a delicate unfolding kimono.

In the *izakaya* section, a row of minimalist free-standing cubes enclose private dining-rooms, their milky translucent cladding lit with pale colours that cycle constantly through the spectrum. Lighting, indeed, is the key to the design, with downlighters and uplighters creating pools of light strategically around stations, tables and on the slopes of the wave ribbon. The limited and subdued palette complements this pattern of lighting, and many of the materials were sourced in Japan, including ebony for the warm wood veneer on the ceiling in a classical *tatami* pattern, and Japanese glass artwork in various installations.

The focal point of the 1400-square-metre underground space is the ribbon installation, suspended from the ceiling, in a pale wood veneer, floating parallel to the main walkway and by the tables.

The lighting design plays a strong role in creating the atmosphere. In the main open area adjacent to the wave installation, the wall is divided by a series of vertical panels that comprise staggered blocks of clear acrylic lit bright red (*right*).

Part of the entrance corridor leading to the *teppanyaki* section of the restaurant is floored with a bed of quartz chips, lined with miniature lights, and covered with plate glass (*below*).

The main entrance corridor (*opposite*), with the simulated 'stream-bed' of quartz along the left, features two large spherical lights made of woven rattan — original in design but in the Japanese style of *midare ami*, meaning 'haphazardly woven'.

Fibre-optic cables illuminate the free-standing small dining-rooms clad in translucent panels, moving slowly through a range of colours (*above*).

A view along the edge of one of the private dining-rooms (*opposite*) towards one of the free-standing dividers; the spaces between the three rooms are also part of the dining area.

{798 Gallery, Beijing} Dashanzi, to the north-east of Beijing on the way to the airport, was for a long time an obscure suburb and a site for state-owned factories, but in recent years, since the closing of much of the production, it has become a new centre for the arts. Indeed, with fewer preconceptions than most cities about fashionable districts, the new market-oriented Beijing is expanding culturally in directions that would be unusual in the West. This area of the city and that around the airport are attracting art galleries and expensive residential apartment blocks rather than industrial parks. For Dashanzi, this began in 2002, with artists and galleries, and more recently boutiques and restaurants, moving into low-rent premises. One of the outstanding spaces was originally Factory 798, making electronics, and built with Soviet aid in the 1950s to an East German architectural and industrial design. Over several decades, it followed the vicissitudes of modern Chinese history, from the Great Leap Forward through the Cultural Revolution, to its final closure. Discovered and opened by photographer Xu Yong, 798 Space is now a gallery for the new boom in Chinese contemporary art, as well as an exhibition space, with another 300 square metres given over to a cafe, art book store and video screening.

Covering 1200 square metres, the huge concrete vaulted-and-ribbed central hall rises to nine metres. The brutalist finish of the interior retains old slogans painted in red — 'Long live Chairman Mao' and 'Great Leader, Great Captain' — and makes an ironic contrast with the experimental but lucrative art hung below.

{Skip House, Kyoto} In the heart of the old residential district of Shimog-amo in north Kyoto, a cut-away cube in white with flashes of orange rises into a stepped wedge overlooking the surrounding older homes toward the hills that mark the edge of the city. This is the Skip House, filling a double lot with a modernist interpretation of the Japanese tradition of interlocking spaces and the interpenetration of indoor and outdoor living. The façade that it presents to the street is all but blank — a white box above a carport — but behind, this multi-generational dwelling reveals a complex variety of spaces that become intelligible only slowly by walking through, around and over them.

There are elements of secrecy and surprise in the many entrances and interconnections that are reminiscent of an old *karakuri* house (constructed with tricks and favoured by *ninja*). These include the dark and narrow staircase that runs up one side of the house, and doorways that open on to different, unexpected parts of the stepped terrace. A deliberate variety of surfaces and textures contributes to the feeling that this is a house made to be explored: floors of slate, wood and *tatami*, ceilings of glass and different finishes of concrete, including the scalloped underside of a flight of steps, and partitions that include the traditional *shoji* but also punched steel and bright orange lacquer.

The complexity of the space is a reflection of the ample time and resources that were available to the Kyoto-based architectural practice, FOBA, under the direction of its founder Katsu Umebayashi. The project took five years to complete. The plot measures just 10 x 20 metres, yet the living experience seems more ample, for five people and three cars, thanks to the variety of spaces and the way in which they interlock. Kyoto is significantly conservative, even by Japanese standards, and many of its neighbours consider the Skip House rather odd, not least because it has and uses a view over the surroundings — unthinkable for most traditional, single-unit dwellings in old urban areas. Nevertheless, it represents a change of direction for the meaning of a house in modern Japan.

From the top level of the terrace, the view takes in the complex variety of courts, levels and material textures. A cylindrical steel balustrade in the foreground is painted the orange colour of traditional *torii* Shinto gates, echoed by the light shining from a window adjoining the brightly coloured *tatami* room on the ground floor.

A sliding orange door, curved to fit the sculpted ceiling, gives access to the corridor leading to the *tatami* room (**opposite left**).

Almost hidden along one wall of the house, a narrow stairway, its steps clad in slate and its walls in polished concrete, leads to the upper-floor bedrooms (**opposite right**).

Seen from the living-room, with its variety of textured surfaces, is one of two interior courtyards, though neither is particularly obvious among the many decks, gaps, enclosures and projections (**left**).

Looking up towards the orange balustrade from the mid-levels of the terrace, the light walls of perforated aluminium sheeting surround the central light-well, and were salvaged from a plant manufacturing tin cans (**above**).

An upstairs bedroom combines traditional textures (the *tatami* mats in blue-green *igusa* straw, though atypically square) with a smoothly curved wall cut with two narrow windows (**below left**).

A scalloped ceiling in the principal living area downstairs rises from a cylinder that encloses a bathroom — one of several tricks of concealment and surprise built into the house (**below right**).

Orange walls and screens surround the non-traditional interpretation of a traditional *tatami* room, which can be used as necessary as a *chashitsu* or tea-ceremony room. Both corridor and room are punctuated by low porthole windows (**overleaf**).

{Biasa Gallery, Bali} A different setting, in an area entirely dependent on international tourism, Seminyak in Bali, hosts another new art gallery, at the same time neutral and distinctive. Biasa Art Space, designed by Italian architect Giovanni d'Ambrosio and completed in 2001, is conceived as a double-height 'container' for a variety of works. The island's unique combination of natural beauty, adapted Hindu traditions and a culture in which arts and crafts play a respected and integral part, have since the 1920s made it pre-eminent in south-east Asian fine arts.

The volume of the gallery and its surfaces are simple, so as to provide a neutral space for the art and a finish that accords with local Balinese technology. The space is governed by three large 'chimneys' that function both as light-wells downwards and for heat transfer upwards. The clean, geometrical lines are maintained by the use of basic raw materials — cement, iron, wood and glass; the single chromatic element is orange. A free staircase in the centre of the building connects the ground and mezzanine levels; this is supported by rusted steel pillars.

The high tropical sun pours vertically down through the double light-wells and reflects from the pale grey tiles (*below*). The orange light fittings are filtered through plastic sheeting of the type widely used by Balinese rice farmers.

The free-standing staircase has steps of deeply polished local hardwood, used also for small block seats scattered around the floor (*right*).

{**Fuchun Resort, Hangzhou**} Completed in 2004, this cluster of villas in the foothills of the Fuchun Mountains, near Hangzhou, is a refined essay in celebrating one of the most elegant periods in Chinese architecture, that of the twelfth-century Southern Sung Dynasty. The twelve villas are part of a hotel and golf-course complex conceived by its owner, a Taiwanese industrialist with a chain of paper factories across China. Passionate about Chinese culture, he engaged Kuala Lumpur-based architect Jean-Michel Gathy to find a modern expression for this style of architecture. It was a key period in Chinese architectural history, of refinement characterized by curved rooflines and the development of crossbeams to support the heavy roofs.

Post-and-beam construction is a building technique long associated with Chinese architecture, and was at its most delicate and open during the Sung period. By using this method, Gathy was able to achieve a notable sensation of open space and light in the interiors. Interior wooden columns support a latticework of crossbeams in an inverted pyramid, supported by short posts and brackets, all of which support the roof, but are left exposed inside. Nowhere is this more effectively used than in the interior swimming-pools attached to each villa, while the hotel itself, below the promontory where the villas are situated, has a main swimming pavilion in this style that is 250 square feet in area.

Another prominent feature of this style of architecture is its axial symmetry, a reflection of the principle of imposing order, on structures as well as society. Gathy adapted the traditional approach through a courtyard by creating two water courts, partly enclosed by plain white walls, and crossed by closely spaced rectangular stepping-stones. The interior finish is elegant and restrained, in polished timber, grey granite, white walls and copper silk. The small community of villas, a template for others being built else-where on the huge property, looks out over the landscaped golf-course and tea plantation towards the south. Fuchun, indeed, was the inspiration for one of the masterpieces of Chinese landscape painting, by the prodigious Huang Gongwang (1269-1354).

Seen from the Fuchun Pavilion, organized for meetings and social functions, the villas are clustered on the brow of a hill (*below*). The location was the inspiration for the horizontal scroll painting 'Dwelling in the Fuchun Mountains', by Huang Gongwang, designated one of the Four Masters of the Yuan period.

The view from the doorway of a villa looks past the outer walls towards the Fuchun Mountains (*opposite above*).

Exposed post-and-beam construction, exemplified here in the old ancestral hall of Bao Lung Ge in Anhui Province, is characteristic of traditional Chinese architecture, and used throughout the villas (*below*).

Each villa has its own spacious indoor swimming-pool. Here, traditionally exposed timber framing is used to its full advantage. The massive teak posts, bedded in granite, carry on their tops an openwork timber structure to support the rafters and beams of a heavy tile roof (*overleaf*).

A hammered metal light fitting decorates the wall of the swimming-pool (*opposite above left*). The living and dining area has exposed post-and-beam timbers (*opposite above right*). The villas feature between one and three bedrooms (*opposite below left*). Sunlight filters through the lattice screens on to a coffee table and sitting area in a corner of the swimming pavilion (*opposite below right*). An antique ceramic vase stands at the end of a villa corridor (*above*). Simplicity of line, polished textures and a palette ranging from creamy-grey to copper evoke the traditional without pastiche.

{Luuk Chang Restaurant, Tokyo} In the conglomeration of malls above Shinjuku station, Tokyo (the world's busiest, with three million passengers a day), is Shunkan, at the top of My City department store. Japan is enjoying a restaurant boom, and this is one of its most concentrated expressions — a two-storey open-plan complex of designer restaurants, each with a striking visual theme, covering a wide variety of cuisines, many of them from other Asian countries (and kitchens frequently open to view). Oriental interpretations of other cultures are somewhat different from the way Westerners generally tackle these things. In creating the styling for the Thai restaurant Luuk Chang ('Baby Elephant' in Thai), designer Tsutomu Kurokawa was inspired by the projected image of Thailand in Japan rather than attempting some reconstructed version of an original Thai restaurant.

In the heart of an ultra-modern restaurant complex above Shinjuku station, mirrors and glass panels evoke 'Thai-ness' through the etching of intricate patterns in green and red (*right*).

The emblem of the restaurant in a red mirror — a baby elephant (*below*), also named in Thai script; the surrounding patterns are derived from the traditional motifs illustrated in the image above.

Thai decorative arts make a significant contribution to traditional architecture: the *kanok* and *krachang* (flame and leaf) motifs, shown here in a detail from a mother-of-pearl door at Bangkok's Grand Palace (*above*), inspired Kurokawa's restaurant design.

Thai Dining

สกุลน้าง
ช LUUK CHANG

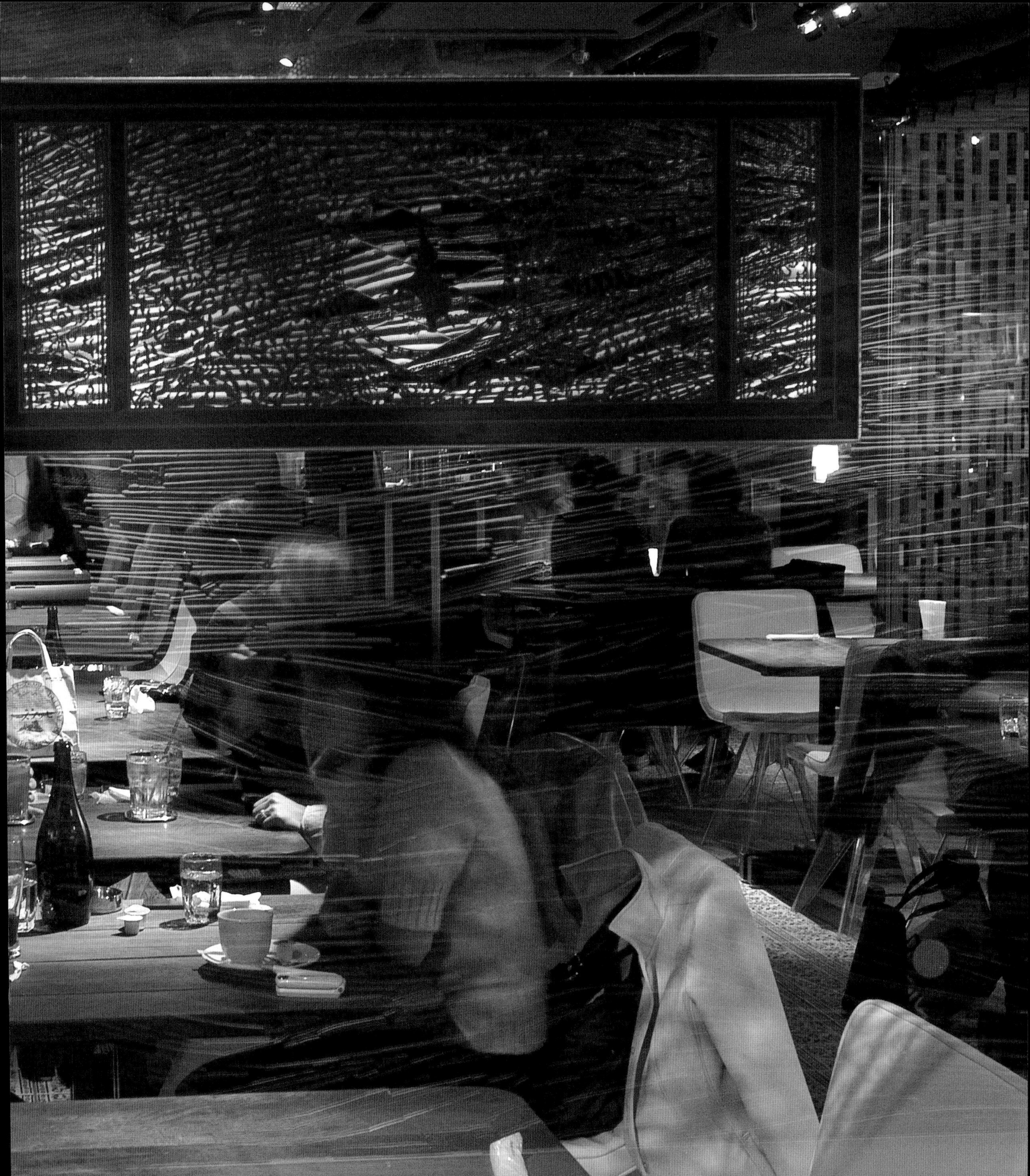

{de Biolley House, Beijing} Close to the Drum Tower in Beijing, an individual form of courtyard dwelling has been converted for modern use, with a Western-style bathroom and a workshop for the owner, Jehanne de Biolley, a jewelry designer. Its high, spacious dimensions are evidence that this was originally part of a temple (indeed, the oldest unrestored temple in the city). The approach, past a warren of workshops and warehouses, shows a newer layer in the urban archaeology of Beijing, as this was more recently part of a factory complex.

The house is arranged around a completely secluded centre, with the entrance a narrow doorway, as usual, tucked away beyond the south-east corner. The courtyard, currently home to a Mongolian yurt for the children to use as a play space, is not simply a private space, but carries the constant traffic between the living-rooms on the north side, the kitchen and dining-room on the south-west, and the jewelry workshop on the east.

Most of the restoration work has been applied to the living-room, bedroom and bathroom areas on the north side. The unusually massive wooden pillars, four metres tall and painted a traditional red, are the principle component of the post-and-beam construction. They are set back one metre from the courtyard-facing wall which, being non-loadbearing, carries a large window surface: the interior of the living-room is therefore much lighter than would be normal in a courtyard house.

The yurt, a light travelling version used for summer pasturing in Mongolia, is such a specialized tented structure that it required Mongolians to erect it here in the courtyard *(below)*.

The main living-room *(right)*, large by the standards of old Beijing courtyard houses, is furnished comfortably and simply, with part of the owner's collection of modern Chinese art.

One of the structural alterations made by the owners
was to connect the different wings of the house with
a corridor (*right*).

All the wooden surfaces, from structural to ledges
and window frames, have been painted bright red.
The load-bearing pillars make large windows
possible (*opposite*).

{**Krung Thai Bank, Bangkok**} Banks in Thailand have never been thought of as places requiring attractive, welcoming interiors, and are almost universally dismal and nondescript. Such architectural effort as has been applied has generally been directed towards overpowering exteriors to reflect corporate self-importance. In a fast-growing economy, boosted by the arrival of international banking groups, this has been seen as a possible area for design improvement. The Krung Thai Bank, a solely government-owned institution, was especially due for a makeover.

As part of updating the bank's image, interior design consultants PIA were responsible for the first serious contemporary design overhaul in the country's banking system with their design for the headquarters on Sukhumvit in Bangkok, completed in 2004. The architects' PAA Studio devised a tall central lobby space around a massive central structural column, and PIA chose this as the focal point of the design. They used sand-blasted glass panels suspended from above to minimize glare from the outer surface of the mirror, also installing 52 kilometres of fibre-optic cables on the column's inner surface, set to cycle through a colour sequence.

The central structural column changes colour constantly, the hues largely based on the bank's corporate colours. The ceiling is laid with stepped squares of aluminium composite, which both animates the upper part of the space, and is a solution to the existing unlevelled ceiling. A chequerboard platform of lit translucent panels on one side of the lobby echoes the colour sequencing in the central column.

{Grosvenor House Apartment, Shanghai}

Shanghai owed its first economic boom to being a Treaty Port open to foreign traders, one result of the 1839-42 Opium War. By the 1920s, the construction of many landmark buildings was under way, as part of the visible signs of the existence of the city's two great trading empires, founded by Sephardic Jewish families from Baghdad and Bombay, the Sassoons and the Hardoons. Heavily influenced by the Art Deco movement in the United States and Europe, buildings on the Bund and elsewhere, such as Sassoon House, the Metropole Hotel, Grosvenor House, the Embankment Building, Hamilton House and Cathay Mansions, gave Shanghai its distinctive character. Grosvenor House was built in 1931 by the Cathay Land Company in imitation of the 1923 Barclay-Vesey Building in New York, though with a lower central tower. The Mayan-inspired Art Deco design of the original by Ralph Walker set the tone, and it always remained one of the smartest residential addresses.

Advertising director Melvyn Chua decided to refurbish the spacious apartment that he took over in the building, with the help of interior and product designer Robert Chan of Nube. Chan made the most of the space available (unusual in Shanghai) by removing interconnecting doors and using a simple, relaxing colour scheme of cream and brown. This carries some of the client's collection of modern Chinese art and fashion photography. The furniture is an integration of modern (some designed by Chan himself), newly-built Art Deco, and traditional Ming.

In the master bedroom, the traditional form of a Chinese canopy bed has been re-interpreted in square-sectioned wood (*below*). A distinctly 'twenties panel (*above*) indicates the age of the apartment.

The living-room (*right*), which opens through at the far end to the dining-room, successfully combines modern, retro and traditional furniture into the Art Deco space. The white fabric-covered seating and black tables were designed by Robert Chan, a Ming cabinet stands in the alcove, and two black leather armchairs are 1950s reproductions.

The place settings for the dining-room were created by Chan — gold-leaf trays and black pebble chopstick holders (*opposite above left*). In the living-room, a set of four white ceramic cubic candleholders stand on a wooden tray (*opposite above right*). Small aluminium bowls and ceramic dishes stand on a living-room table (*opposite below left*). Modern lacquering for the dining table includes golden teacups and coppery finish to a square teapot (*opposite below right*). The spacious proportions of the 1930s apartment allow for a modern dining table in the form of a massive slab of wood that can seat eight or ten people. The alcove has been filled with three vases used to hold thick candles. At right is the owner's collection of modern fashion photography (*above*).

{Red Capital Residence, Beijing} Beijing's lanes, with their courtyard houses, have been a characteristic part of the city's fabric since the Han Dynasty, though now fast disappearing under the explosive growth of the new market-led economy. The feelings among the people who live or have lived there are mixed. For some, the close community spirit is something that will be missed, while for others the ridding of the inconveniences will be welcome. The evident increase in the number of public lavatory facilities around the lanes is a reminder that some of the creature comforts that most city-dwellers take for granted do not exist in traditional dwellings.

One restored *siheyuan* is the Red Capital Residence, operated as a boutique hotel. As originally built and conceived, the principal rooms were on the north side, facing south into the sunlight. The entrance, typically, is offset slightly from the south-east corner of the quadrangle so that the courtyard is not visible from the lane. Surrounded by a masonry wall, the small complex of buildings follows the basic principles of the courtyard house, namely timber post-and-beam construction with non-loadbearing partition walls between rooms, and the extension of the dwelling into the garden.

On the north-west side of the small complex, a tiny 'corner courtyard' gives access to one secluded bedroom, with an old four-post canopy bed (*below*).

The bedrooms on three sides and the sitting-room and bar on the other face into a small central courtyard (*right*), which is enlivened by a poplar and a small rock garden clustered at its base. The rocks conceal the tiny entrance to a former bomb shelter, which Beijing residents were ordered to build during the Cold War. This has been converted into an intimate, if claustrophobic bar.

{Tiandiyijia, Beijing} On Nan Chi Zi Street, right next to Beijing's Forbidden City, and overlooking the old Imperial Archives, this restored and internally re-modelled old mansion in grey stone is now an elegant restaurant, Tian Di Yi Jia. The original central courtyard has been roofed over in glass, and the lighting modulated through suspended inverted paper umbrellas; in the evening these glow a luminous yellow. On the north side of the courtyard an upper floor gives on to a balcony, and here the designers have fitted a water feature in the form of a wide stone slope at table height, carved with ripples across which a sheet of water flows into a trough at the lower end. The private rooms on this upper floor give on to a terrace which overlooks the Imperial Archives and is subdivided by free-standing slab walls, inset with antique carved openwork pillars.

The upper floor of one wing of the property has two bays with tables, and a massive stone tray set at a gentle gradient, its surface carved to give the impression of ripples in sand. Water flows from the long gap at left and across the rippled surface, on which are set candles.

What was originally the central courtyard (*overleaf*) has been roofed over with a raised skylight to create the main restaurant area. Paper umbrellas are hung upside-down under the glass, as shade during the middle of the day, and for illumination in the evening (each is fitted with an electric lamp).

The terrace, accessed from the private dining-rooms, looks out on to the former Imperial Archives. The space is divided by stone walls which contain at each end antique columns (*above left*).

The upper floor, hung with old lanterns, has a sitting area at right, while at left are private dining-rooms that each give on to the terrace shown at left (*above*).

{Taman Mertasari, Bali} A compound of five housing complexes surrounds a large communal garden dotted with trees and palms, in a backwater of Sanur, one of the older resort districts of Bali. The most distinctive buildings are three tall rice granaries called *lumbung*, traditional to the island and here used as sleeping accommodation and as a library. *Lumbung* designs vary regionally, and these are from this southern part of the island. Balconies have been added to them, while the original function of the pillars and their broad wooden discs was to stop rodents from entering.

One of the three *lumbung*, dismantled and removed from their original Balinese domestic settings and re-built in the compound, is now used as a library. Its protective stilted design now helps to conserve books instead of rice (*left*).

Another *lumbung* is used as a guest bedroom for one of the five properties around the perimeter of the compound, overlooking a central pond (*below*).

{2. Space}

Two features stand out in Oriental conceptual approaches to space – the way it is divided, and the relationship between interior and exterior. These are by no means consistent, but there are common threads running through the several cultures, and some principles have been found powerful enough to have spread. The influences on these approaches to space management are a mixture of the practical, such as climate and shortage of land, the cultural and the aesthetic.

The division of an interior by means of lightweight partitions occurs as one all-pervasive theme, and was originally possible because of building techniques that did not rely on load-bearing walls and used relatively light materials, particularly wood. Post-and-beam construction originated in China, and within this framework there came flexibility in the way the space it enclosed could be used. In Japan, the use of lightweight sliding screens, both *shoji* (translucent paper on a light frame) and *fusuma* (solid wood) made re-arrangement of space simple and normal. Modern construction methods and new materials have made it possible to expand and develop the concept of multi-use interiors.

Intimately linked to the way in which spaces are closed off or opened up is the understanding of the interpenetration of indoor and outdoor. The courtyard houses illustrated in the opening section of this book have been tremendously influential in the way they demonstrate ways of managing limited space and of reconciling the needs of privacy and openness. The garden, in many ways essential to a sense of well-being, is imported into the house, even though it may contain no more than a single tree — or not even that in the austere, Zen-influenced dry gardens of Japan. As Werner Blaser writes in *The Courtyard House in China*, 'Enclosure and opening in one is the fundamental principle', this type of dwelling is 'invested with a feeling for usefulness and a potent symbolism.' A traditional variation on this single-storey, four-sided aggregation is a two-storey building with an open light-well in the middle, as in the Ming and Qing merchants' houses of Anhui. The largely blank walls present a sealed face to the outside world, but the interior is animated by the openings that face each other across the court; light flooding downwards creates a very particular atmosphere.

Another fundamental aspect of the Oriental manipulation of architectural space is the weakening of the boundaries between interior and exterior, so that one flows into the other, an effect achieved by projecting floors, verandas and terraces, and by the arrangement of dwelling units into an interconnected cluster

with open walkways, as in traditional Thai houses. Tropical and sub-tropical weather conditions encourage this approach to building, which may also involve moveable partitions. This blurring of boundaries tends to inspire certain perceptual ambiguities. One classic device of garden design, 'borrowed landscape', for instance, takes a painter's perspective to construct a view from a specific point that harmoniously balances foreground, middle distance and background — but with the background being outside the property. The composition is organized so that this is not obvious and the perspective is compressed. One of the houses in this section takes an intriguing modern approach to this form of space management by illusion. This is one form of controlling and framing a view, and there are other examples of this approach here, all with the underlying aim of orchestrating the experience of space.

The ovoid Sunfish House (*opposite left*) by Satoshi Okada in Atami, Japan, clad in the traditional copper plates used for temple roofs.

Bentwood seat and footrest by Yoko Matsumura (*opposite right*).

The atrium lobby of a beach house in Hua Hin, Thailand, by Architects 49 (*below left*).

Pond and garden run the length of the Kong House in Bali, by Ian Chee (*below right*).

{Lotus House, Kanagawa, nr. Tokyo} Built in 2005 in a steep wooded valley in Kanagawa, south of Tokyo, the Lotus House represents the development of a theme that the architect, Kengo Kuma, has been pursuing for some time — the construction of open, porous buildings: 'I thought of filling water between the house, and planting lotus so that the dwelling would be conveyed by the lotus to the river, and continue into the woods on the other side.'

The pursuit of a porous, lightweight building style has a deeper purpose for Kuma than simply employing materials in new ways. It is both an attempt to get away from the monumentalism of the twentieth century and to replace the ideal of the house as a sturdy bulwark of security with a gentler, more delicate solution sympathetic to the environment. Integral to the success of this search was finding the right structural medium. Five years earlier, Kuma had had particular success with his Stone Museum in the Tochigi prefecture, a project that required him to find ways of working with local grey andesite that would make it appear slim, light and soft. He achieved this through a method of de-construction aimed at 'transparent' stone walls. In one version the stone was cut into thin slats to create horizontally arranged 'stone louvres'; in a second, a porous wall was made from blocks laid in staggered courses and then a third of them removed. Here, in the Lotus House, the stone chosen was travertine cut into thin plates 20 cm x 60 cm and 3 cm thick. An even lighter and more porous effect was made possible by suspending them in a chequerboard pattern on flat steel bars 8 x 16 mm thick. As Kuma puts it, 'an expression of the lightness of lotus petals using stone.'

The site, deep in the hills, is by a small, quiet river, and the house, which is very large by Japanese standards, is composed of two wings, each of two storeys. These are linked by a deep, roofed terrace that faces a broad reflecting pool with lotuses.

In an effort to create what he terms 'weak' architecture, Kengo Kuma based much of the construction on open walls of thin travertine slabs (**above**). Travertine, a fine-grained form of limestone, is itself porous in its composition, with natural holes and crevices.

The visitor's first view of the house is from a walkway on the upper level, across a reflecting pool. Although the material is massive stone, the walls are ambiguous (**opposite**).

Seen from across the lotus pond, the steep slope behind the building partly encloses the back of the terrace so that it becomes not quite open-air but neither a room in the normal sense. The upper open wall allows the wind to sweep through.

In the ground-floor living-room, a sliding wall close by the entrance reveals or encloses a choice of either a statue of Buddha in its alcove or a plasma screen, with no irony intended (*opposite*).

An upper-level bathroom offers two stone tubs, one in the open air, the other enclosed in glass for colder weather, looking out over the hills (*above*). The reflections of the adjacent travertine wall in the glass walls, and the mirror-like siting of the tubs, enhance the illusion of transparency.

{Vadanyakul House, Bangkok} The traditional central Thai dwelling, known as a *reuan thai*, is quite intimately connected to its environment, at least when ideally located in the shade of trees. Constructed entirely of wood, it is raised high on pillars, and comprises a number of buildings connected by open terraces. Family life is largely conducted outdoors and on sheltered verandas, surrounded by trees wherever possible.

Architect Prabhakorn Vadanyakul wanted to find a way to maintain this connection between dwelling and the exterior habitat, while designing a space for himself and his wife that suits a twenty-first-century lifestyle. He had always grown up with trees and wished to maintain that connection, particularly as his father had planted the family plot, in the northern part of Bangkok, with seeds from around the country. The site has every aspect of a jungle of mature tropical trees. At the same time, Vadanyakul appreciates the mechanical/technological aesthetic, and is, in his own words, 'obsessed' with aviation (both he and his wife are pilots). The result, in this award-winning house, is the unlikely but wholly successful combination of mechanical playground and forest-viewing platform. Vadanyakul says, 'I want to show that nature and technology are not polar issues. In other words, we can choose to live both, without excluding one from the other.'

Thai architecture maintains a long tradition of integration with trees and nature, as exemplified by this northern Thai timber house.

The entrance area displays the architect-owner's love of technology, and in particular aeronautical engineering, from the main door at right in the form of an aircraft wing, to the steps in the shape of wing sections. The kitchen-dining area and rear terrace lie beyond.

The staircase, supported on a single diagonal beam, rises up one side of the house, but stepping around it one finds a glass-floored reading area that seems to project into the surrounding forest (*opposite*).

The living area at the rear of the house (*above*) includes kitchen, dining and seating in open plan, allowing the maximum impression of surrounding nature. The floor is of local, polished white sandstone.

Heavy wheels (*opposite above left*) attached to one end of the rear glass wall run along a circular track to allow it to be swung completely open (*above*). Open ducting in the study-cum-workshop (*opposite above right*), used mainly for modelmaking and computers, makes it the most machine-like space in the house. As the owner explains, 'The house is scattered with airplane parts and several other aerodynamic forms', here a bench in the shape of a wing section (*opposite below left*). Tensioned steel cables are used to support a variety of elements around the house, from the staircase here (*opposite below right*) to toilet paper rolls in the bathroom. A massive steel-and-glass end wall on the ground floor rolls away on an overhead curved track to open the house entirely to the terrace and swimming-pool (*above*).

The almost total transparency, with glass on all sides, brings the forest into all corners of the house, as here in the master bedroom at the rear (*above*), but at the same time the trees ensure privacy.

The steel-framed house, seen here from the swimming-pool (*opposite*), was conceived with the site in mind, and fits into a slot between the trees, which press around it. The architect writes, 'Although the physical aspects of this house are in contrast with its surrounding, it shows a great respect to nature.'

{Kong House, Bali} In a developing area of Bali in Seminyak, in the south of the island, the Singaporean owner of a plot of land wanted a holiday property that was open, convenient to live in, and yet maintained some references to traditional Balinese dwellings (though not at all overtly). The site was originally virgin paddy fields, and though close to the sea, there was no possibility of a view from the single-storey structure, which was also what the client requested. Architect Ian Chee has designed a complex that creates entirely its own habitat within the surrounding walls. Chee's intention was to re-interpret the traditional Balinese layout of a dwelling. In this, there is a series of small constructions grouped in the same compound, with a minimum of five areas: entrance, bedroom, kitchen, bathroom and granary. The precise layout varies according to status and caste, and follows rules laid down in treatises, some going back to the fifteenth century. Masonry platforms are traditional, as is the interpenetration of interior and exterior space.

This house, completed in 2004 and with a total built-up area of 550 square metres, was conceived as a series of *bales* (the Balinese version of a gazebo) linked by a covered walkway and orientated to take advantage of the prevailing winds, using large cantilevered overhangs and plated pergolas for shade and protection from rain.

By adapting the arrangement of a traditional Bali home, the architect was able to satisfy the client's wish to keep the guest quarters separate, and these were located in a line extending from the corner housing the kitchen, service quarters and garage. The living shelter followed by the master room extends from this corner at a right angle, while the house temple was placed facing the sacred mountain Gunung Agung in the opposite corner of the compound.

One entire wall of the compound is lined by plantings of small trees (**below**), which border a long pond. The water connects the living area at right with the bathrooms that adjoin the master and second bedrooms.

The focus of the house is the living shelter, roofed but open on three sides. In the centre of this is the sunken seating area, into which steps lead down from two opposite corners (**right**).

Early morning sunlight streams into the living shelter (**overleaf**), with its dining table at left (the kitchen is behind the camera). The area faces out on to the lawn, swimming-pool and a small *bale* in traditional style, thatched with *alang alang* grass.

One of the bedrooms seen from its small courtyard garden (*opposite above*), planted with Bird of Paradise plants (*Strelitzia reginae*). The garden, which can be entered through sliding glass doors, connects the bedroom to the bathroom.

The same bedroom is seen from its entrance (*opposite below*), a full-height sliding door that can open the room fully to the rest of the compound. The living shelter is in the background.

The bathroom of another bedroom seen from its courtyard garden (*below*); open-air bathing is another Balinese tradition that suits the climate. A mirror running the entire width of the bathroom enhances its open, natural aspect.

As the architect comments, 'In material terms, we chose a palette of simple finishes', and in the bathrooms the combination is of river pebbles set in one wall, wood, concrete and polished metal. A borderless mirror, projecting slightly to accommodate concealed lighting behind, gives a modern contrast to the pebbles (*above*). Woven bamboo matting in various forms is used for cupboards and screens (*opposite above left*). A bathroom door-handle is cast in metal from one of the river pebbles used throughout the house (*opposite above right*). A dressing-room mirror, designed by the architect, is set in the neck of a tailor's dummy (*opposite below left*). The imprint of bamboo matting has been left in a concrete ceiling from the formwork (*opposite below right*).

{Asian Gate House, Okinawa} *Shakkei* is the word, Japanese taken from the Chinese, now used to describe the ancient technique of 'borrowed landscape', in which a precisely organized view takes its distant elements from beyond the house and garden. It is both a form of illusion that extends the space and an art form. Early Kyoto gardeners had to work hard to 'capture the view alive' as the older term *ikedori* had it, partly by siting, but more by framing the view in various ways, such as planting to hide what was not visually required. In the contemporary world, this device is more difficult to use, as the landscape is subject to unpredictable and unsightly changes: for instance, the presence of power lines and high-rise apartment blocks.

On the island of Okinawa, architect Tetsuo Goto and his client Amon Miyamoto, theatre and film director, have made a modern version of *shakkei* the central theme of this house. The level limestone formations on this side of the island form wide, flat bays ringed by low, undercut cliffs. They chose the location of the house carefully, on the edge of a cliff, looking out to sea and the distant headland, site of the ruins of the castle of Tamagusku. The house is positioned in front of one of the island's many distinctive rock formations — a massive boulder of Ryukyuan limestone carved by wave action. A broad wooden terrace extends out over the edge of the cliff, its two wings enclosing a view of the rock from the living-room. The illusion makes it seem quite modest in size and located at the end of the terrace, whereas it is actually the size of a house and more than a hundred metres offshore. All around it, the limestone bedding is so flat that the tide recedes completely twice a day, thus constantly changing the framed views of landscape and seascape.

The siting and design of the house is focused on 'capturing' the limestone rock. A rectangular frame to the living-room opens through a series of glass shutters that can rotate individually and slide to one side on runners. The two projections of the wooden terrace enclose the rock, which from here seems much smaller and nearer than it really is (*left*).

Borrowed landscape techniques originated in China, and one of the best-known exemplars is in Zhuozheng Yuan in Suzhou, where a distant pagoda has been brought into the carefully constructed view (*above*).

The *chashitsu*, or tea-ceremony room, makes a second surprising use of the rock. In this radical re-design of a traditional space, the scroll painting which normally occupies the alcove, and is typically either calligraphy or a Chinese-style mountain-water landscape, has been replaced by a narrow window, which reveals part of the rock in the style of such a painting (*above*). Seen from the left side of the house, a small reflecting pool also 'captures' the seascape by reflection, the rock appears at left (*opposite above right*). A covered concrete corridor leads down to the edge of the small cliff, for a view of the reflecting pool (*opposite below left*). In the tea-ceremony room, the usual flower arrangement is replaced by a circular lacquered depression in the ledge in front of the narrow window, filled with water in which a single orchid floats (*opposite above left* and *below right*).

In addition to capturing the rock, another aspect of the 'borrowed landscape' is the continually changing appearance of the bay, here seen at high tide in the afternoon (*above*). Two *tokkuriyashi* palms (*Mascarena lagenicaulis*), named after the *tokkuri*, or Japanese sake bottle, add symmetry and a stronger sense of enclosing the rock.

Because of the almost flat limestone bedding off-shore, the tide recedes several hundred metres, revealing a totally different. almost dry, seaweed-strewn landscape at low-tide (*above*).

{House in Hua Hin, Gulf of Thailand} Since the early twentieth century, Hua Hin on the Gulf of Thailand, originally a summer retreat for royalty and the court, has been a restrained, quiet resort. In 1924, King Vajiravudh (Rama VI) had built the Mareukatayawan Palace a little way along the coast, and in 1929 Rama VII had another palace constructed, called Klai Kangwon ('Far from Cares'). Because of the associations with royalty (the present king spends lengthy periods there), this place has none of the brashness and entertainment excesses of Pattaya on the opposite side of the Gulf and of Patong on Phuket. Hua Hin is particularly popular with people seeking weekend homes. Beach frontage property is in short supply, and a plot here is often long and narrow. In this case, the client required a modern weekend villa that made maximum visual use of its small beach frontage and yet also gave range to the old Thai principle of building in linked units, with a variety of internal and external spaces. In addition, the architects and client agreed that understated references should be made to the colonial style of the early Hua Hin properties, by incorporating courts and some interior oval spaces.

The architects, A49 Limited, arranged the accommodation and services into three units of different sizes, or 'pavilions', along the narrow 1800-square-metre site. The service pavilion is closest to the road, linked by a grass court to the principal, three-storey sleeping pavilion. Plantings and a water court link this in turn to a largely transparent communal pavilion that serves as a living- and dining-room. A pathway continues from here to the beach. The interior of the main unit, finished in white, wood and glass, has striking spatial variety and carefully organized views from different levels towards the beach and sea. The experience of entering and walking through the long axis is designed so that nature, simplicity and the sea gradually unfold with the succession of views and spaces.

A spacious double-height reception area looks straight down the axis of the complex, while a curved staircase flows up one side (*these pages*). Plain white walls were chosen for simplicity and to avoid the problem of fading due to saline humidity.

The tradition of beach properties began in 1924 with the building of the Mareukatayawan Palace for King Rama VI in British colonial style (*opposite*).

The master bedroom on the top floor has a panorama on three sides, and opens on to a roof terrace facing the sea (*overleaf*).

The communal pavilion, closest to the beach, has sliding glass panels that can be fully opened to give it maximum exposure to the sea-view and the water body running along one side (*left*). Electrically operated blinds can compensate for the glare of the strong midday sun.

The main building at dusk looms over the water court and an area of plantings that help to soften its angular geometry (*below*).

One corner of the study complex is designed as an oasis of quiet simplicity (*these pages*). Water falls from a ledge of coral limestone into a sunken pool with carp; next to it is a low bench carved from a solid block of Wenge hardwood.

{Forest Study, Singapore} Singapore's widely publicized greening policy, implemented since the 1976 formation of the Parks and Recreation Department, has succeeded in creating a tropical garden city, despite increasing urbanization. The sense of living with nature is expected and usual, but in this office, located in the grounds of the owner's house, architect Ko Shiou Hee took the principle much further. As he says, 'The notion of the rigorously composed architectural form takes a backseat.' In its place is an assembly of naturally crafted spaces partitioned by stone and glass, a response to the client's request for a study that would incorporate surrounding nature, be separate from the house and largely unseen from it.

Walkways weave between vegetation of differing species; rooms are surrounded by trees and ferns in every tropical shade of green; light enters as it would in nature — sometimes creating chiaroscuro effects as the tropical sun filters through the leaves; at other times it is soft and diffused. Ko wanted to go beyond the conventional architectural experience of a principally visual aesthetic, to include sound, touch and smell. Forest Study invites the experience of a stroll through captured forest space, with bird calls, trickling water and the aroma of the undergrowth. It begins with a path that winds around the perimeter of the grounds, crossing a small wooden bridge, down a lane of vegetation and across stepping-stones to the glass entrance. The existing shrubs, ferns and trees were left in place and determined the order of the architectural units, while the principal materials were chosen to enhance the natural ambience — black-flamed granite, yellow rustic bush-hammered stone (both from China) and pink coral stone from Spain, with dark wood for walls, cabinets and fittings.

Massive granite alternates with glass to form a structure that appears from inside to move in and out of the enclosing forest. The view here is from the entrance to the owner's private study in the background (*above*).The path leading to the study begins at the main entrance to the house, first crossing a small bridge and then turning to the left to weave through tropical vegetation (*opposite above left*). In keeping with the client's brief, the study complex is embedded in greenery, with no façade as such, only partly revealed as fragments of stone wall and glass (*opposite below left*). A meeting room next to the study entrance sets the tone for visitors of a natural space intertwined with nature. The rough stone wall extends past the frameless glass of the window to heighten the sense of connection with the forest (*opposite above right*). A continuation of the path, set irregularly in a pebble bed, passes the tennis court which the architect has concealed from view with a wooden wall (*opposite below right*).

Around two sides of the tall glass-walled private study is an aviary, its mesh fence concealed within the vegetation. Cloth sails deflect direct sunlight from the owner's work table, in solid oak from the furniture company E15 (*opposite*).

On the other side of the study is a natural aquarium, where the glass wall cuts a vertical cross-section through a pond. Concealed metal halide downlighters illuminate the water (*above*).

{Soi 38 House, Bangkok } Central Bangkok is an unusual mixture of new high-rise commercial properties and old residential neighbourhoods secreted away in warrens of narrow lanes, called *soi* (a number of these were formerly canals). The scale of these residential areas ranges between slum and old landed property, the majority of all of this still one- or two-storey dwellings. This large family house, completed in 2002 by the award-winning Bangkok architectural practice A49, occupies 2,000 square metres near the end of one of the *soi* that winds south from one of the principal downtown streets, Sukhumvit. By the standards of this relatively well-off neighbourhood, the plot is a little confined, the more so given the client's request for a very full specification of spaces, including a large karaoke room, swimming-pool and exercise gym — effectively requiring a four-storey house.

Moreover, while the client was not looking for any traditional Thai forms or spatial organization, he did have specific demands that the structure and layout conform to the principle of *feng shui*. This Chinese form of geomancy, often presented in the West in a rather bowdlerized fashion, is always site-specific and esoteric. In this case, the *feng shui* master had been involved even before the architects, and his indications were a part of the brief. They included specifications that the house should face south (unusually), that the dwelling should lie against the north-east corner of the plot, and that the layout should conform to a nine-part division of the land, with the entrance to be in part number eight and the master bedroom to be the dominant feature.

The main issues, therefore, were to keep the mass light in appearance and to combine modernist design with a traditional framework. The solution was a structure of what appear to be light, open, interpenetrating boxes, with two of them projecting quite strongly. This articulation masks the fact that there are actually four storeys, while the use of white concrete with a large window area enhances the feeling of lightness.

Looking down from the first-floor bedroom balcony on to the swimming-pool and private gymnasium; these are housed separately.

The view from the end of the swimming-pool, which occupies almost the full length of the plot: the articulation of the structure above the water and the openings in the high wall are designed to lighten the appearance of the massive house (*above*).The staircase spans four storeys including the basement, and the deep well is illuminated by vertical windows on two sides. An elongated artwork fits the space between the second and third floors (*opposite left*). Openings in walls, such as this divider between the swimming-pool area and the court in front of the entrance, discover views around the property (*opposite above far right*). The swimming-pool continues as a water body and divider between the main house and the gymnasium, which is reached by slate-capped stepping-stones (*opposite below far right*).

At dusk, the projecting cubes that comprise the house appear to float (*above*). The living-room unit, occupying the corner closest to the entrance, has two of its walls made entirely in glass.

Floor-to-ceiling glass walls at the entrance and along one corridor help to give a light and airy impression on entering the house (*opposite above*). At strategic points, carefully chosen pieces of traditional Thai art and craft are set off against the white, angular modernism — here an Ayutthaya-style cabinet with tapering sides and gold-leaf decoration on the doors.

A vivid blue sets the tone for a dedicated karaoke room at basement level, which opens on to its own sunken courtyard garden at left (*opposite below*).

{House in Kinugasa, Kyoto} Completed in late 2003, this single-storey dwelling in the north-west part of Kyoto is a thoroughly modern interpretation of the traditional Japanese principle of flexibility of space. The owner, a single man about to retire from his position as a professor at a nearby university, was replacing the old family house, and wanted a space that would harmoniously link garden and interior, with the easy possibility of re-arranging the configuration of rooms. Architects Yumi Kori and Toshiya Endo of Studio Myu divided the plot into four principal areas — an entrance based on the traditional *genkan*, the entire interlocking living interior, an enclosed formal garden and the surrounding informal garden with its existing natural plantings, dominated by Cryptomeria (Japanese cedar) and Katsura (a deciduous broadleaf) trees. Sliding doors (*fusuma*) and sliding paper screens (*shoji*) allow almost any combination of these spaces to be linked or divided, and there are views of one or the other garden from everywhere.

For visits of the owner's mother, the entire dwelling can also be re-configured, or at least treated as a tea-ceremony space. This begins with the path from the front wooden gate around the house, which functions as the *roji* (the path along which visitors prepare themselves for the occasion and leave behind the mundane), and the entrance proper to the house, which can function as the *chumon* or 'middle gate', beyond which is the spiritual world of tea.

In a house designed to harmonize garden and interior, the *chashitsu*, or tea-ceremony room, is both modern in its arrangement of planes, and traditional in the way it addresses the interplay of interior darkness and exterior brightness. The low entrance from the small garden beyond is the *nijiri-guchi* or 'wriggling-in entrance', which demands humility to enter.

A small garden of great simplicity adjoins the main living-room, with a single maple, here in autumn at its best colour. This garden plays a role in the tea ceremony for, having entered the house, the guest can step down into the garden and cross to the tiny low entrance in the far left corner, where a single stone is placed for the purpose (*opposite*).

A small anteroom, with a floor of diamond tiles, gives a deliberately limited but exquisitely framed view of the small garden and the stepping-stones that lead down into it (*above*).

Sliding glass panels in wooden frames reinforce the *shoji* paper screens, and both can slide back to open the house all the way through, both visually and physically (***above***).

Shoji screens of handmade paper, stretched across light wooden frames in a modern design of horizontal panels, allow the house to be closed, opened or sub-divided according to taste. This view from the entrance emphasizes the *genkan*, the lower level from which one steps up into the dwelling proper (***right***).

{The Hayama, Kanagawa, Japan} On the winding coast road in Kanagawa prefecture, this narrow, V-shaped plot of land at one end of the main street of the small town of Hayama formerly held a bookshop. When the owners retired, their daughter, an art director in Tokyo, decided to build her house there. Coincidentally, the architect she chose, Kohei Sato, knew the site well from childhood, and had always been keen to find a suitable way of building on it.

Its prominent position encouraged Sato to make a landmark there; having initially considered wood and plaster finishes, the architect decided to emphasize its verticality with a wraparound cladding of red cedar, treated with a patented finish to turn it a mature silver-grey. Inside, the problem was how to create as much openness as possible in a dwelling that had to be arranged vertically. Sato's solution was to open the staircase with various devices to link the different floors. Fitting into a light-well, the staircase, with expanded steel steps, allows light to reach the ground floor relatively unobstructed. The reinforced glass on the steps reflects the sky as one descends the staircase, while glass walls to the stairwell also expand the sense of space.

The brief for the interior design included the need to incorporate the owner's collection of Art Deco and post-modern furniture and other items. Her only stipulation for the colour scheme was a particular shade of magenta-red as a key colour, and this appears in the ground-floor entrance, bedroom and bathroom (and in the living-room in the furniture). Sato complemented this with a pale-cream finish to the walls. The client also wanted a 'loose', relaxed feeling; as a means of achieving this, Sato took pains to make sure that the plastering was given a rough and uneven finish to mask the perfectly smooth plasterboard.

Planks of red cedar, laid vertically, clad the entire exterior of this tall, narrow house. A patented weathering treatment turns the wood a silvery grey.

Three aspects of The Hayama show how the architect has played a kind of counterpoint to the site plan (*right* and *opposite*). Where the triangular plot, at the intersection of two small streets, has its apex, the building is at its most curved, while the sharp 'prow' of the house faces obliquely backwards. The unexpected configuration of one curved side and two straight, and their placement, give the exterior a sculptural quality. An original Mini occupies the small garage that adjoins the entrance to the house (*below*).

Throughout the house, great attention is paid to giving as open and as expansive a feeling as possible in the limited space, and to distributing the light. The third floor is the principal living area, with access to a small roof terrace (*above*). A small study fits into the corner angle, which has been cut away to create a triangular window (*opposite*).

{Khai House, Singapore} In the Khai House in Singapore, Ko Shiou Hee and his architectural practice K2LD worked within the context of an open 'garden' dwelling to create a clear separation of functions without resorting to conventional dividers. The structure, on a corner plot, is formed from two interlocking forms at right angles to each other, and within this, activity spaces are distinguished from service spaces by the arrangement of levels — bedrooms on the upper level, activity areas on ground level and utility quarters in the basement.

Ko's approach to spatial definition is most vigorously pursued at ground level, where there are spaces but with no trace of rooms bounded by walls. Physically, the delineation between the inside and the outside is blurred by sliding glass panels that open the floor completely to the garden, and by the combination of stone, wood, concrete and timber screens that gently prompt the eye to carve out notional spaces and enclosures in what is an open ground plan without walls or a clear boundary line. The garden design pays careful attention to the various framed views *through* the ground floor, such as in a vertical landscape wall next to the pool used as a device to blur the distinction between the horizontal ground plane and the boundaries of the enclosure. The effect is that ground-level spaces open and flow seamlessly into the surrounding landscape. While there is no apparent clarity of spatial segregation, there is a notional sense of spatial distinctiveness — a separation of space that is intuitive more than physical.

The deep overhang of the roof to the single-storey section of the house creates a sheltered deck space which gives shade during the day and protection from rain (*left*).

The T-shaped plan, evident from this corner of the plot, gives prominence to the ground-level living and activity areas (*above*).

Tall wooden 'sails' by the entrance rotate on their vertical mounts to control the airflow (*opposite above left*). Storage and washroom spaces built into the end of the single-storey unit (seen on the previous pages) have doors of sliced rough granite mounted on steel (*opposite above right*). More granite, hand-cut and chiselled in China, is used for the wall at the entrance (*opposite below left*). The oblique cuts and relief recall Inca techniques.Grass dominates the garden, and the plantings are minimalist and sculptural, including small boulders, all with an eye to framing the many views that take in interior and exterior together (*opposite below right*). Louvred wooden screens and glass panels slide to one side to expose the living-room totally to the surroundings when wanted, and Singapore's equatorial climate allows this often (*above*). The acrylic Ox Chair is by Eric Jorgensen.

The plate-glass end of the swimming-pool; on the left, the grass continues up a sloping wall to soften the boundaries of the garden (*below*).

Because of the contours of the land, the site has been levelled by cutting into the slope at right, and to obscure the break, the wall has been planted to give a smooth continuation of green (*opposite above*).

A reverse view through the living-room from that on page 129, from the swimming-pool out towards the main entrance. Again, the framed views are calculated. The table in the centre of the room is a solid block of hardwood from the Indonesian island of Lombok (*opposite below*).

{Sheep Pen, Tokyo} Designed by Japanese architect Yoko Matsumura as a studio and daytime-living space for herself and for entertaining friends, this tiny building is elevated to have the view of a tree-house, and achieves an intimate inter-connection between inside and outside. The available space was in fact extremely limited — no more than that directly above the parking area for a single car at the entrance to the family house — but the garden was special. It contained two old gingko trees, both listed and protected, and a huge camphor tree. In the seemingly endless sub-division of lots, due in large measure to the country's inheritance tax laws designed to eliminate large landholdings, the preservation of large trees such as these is unusual outside temple precincts, but in this area of a Tokyo suburb, the extended family retained ownership of the sub-divisions and was therefore able to keep this old pocket of greenery.

Matsumura wanted a space that was relaxing and refreshing, despite its small dimensions (38 square metres); even though she calls it a 'shed', it has a perfectly framed view of the trees and nothing else. The water supply is concealed in the space between the flat ceiling and the gently curved shell-like roof and within the rear bookcase unit. Behind this unit is a small kitchen space and bathroom. It was named the Sheep Pen after the Chinese zodiacal year in which it was conceived, and the architect's birth-year.

The floor-to-ceiling sliding glass doors open up the entire east side, and at this elevation the view is a solid frame of greenery. The bentwood chair and stool (the latter can also be used as an armrest when seated on the floor) are the architect's own design.

Steel steps lead up to this single opening and its triangular concrete step from the base of the old gingko trees just outside (*left*).

Seen from the rear, which is the normal entrance of the family house (*above*), the building is also a garage for the car beneath.

{House in Sakakida, Kyoto} The city of Kyoto, once the undisputed focus of Japan's cultural heritage, has undergone a relentless erosion of its urban fabric, to the point where, as architect Satoshi Okada puts it, 'The old townscape, a series of magnificent houses, has almost disappeared. Houses in Kyoto today have already little historical context in terms of materiality, tactility in space, and even building forms.' The reasons for this are several, including a pervasive 'intermingling with kitsch and the eclectic' and the more practical safety regulations that disallow all-wood construction. Nevertheless, the owner had asked for a contemporary house that still reflected the spatiality of the old city, and Okada drew on his own experiences of the traditional Kyoto *machiya* style of long, constrained row-house, including 'the essence of dimness and narrowness'.

The immediate distinction of this corner-plot house is its black exterior. The architect explains that black was once a common finish for Kyoto dwellings, which used burnt Japanese cedar timbers (the controlled burning was a form of fireproofing). Fire regulations prevent this today, but Okada used compressed cement panels painted charcoal grey. The tall outer wall ensures privacy for the deep garden, accessible from the ground-floor rooms and viewable from the first-floor (US 2nd) living and dining area. The living-room and kitchen surround on two sides a second courtyard with a wooden deck, and the combination of these two internal open areas follows a traditional *machiya* cooling technique for Kyoto's hot, humid summers. The upper courtyard with its wooden floor heats up in sunlight, and the temperature differential between this and the cooler garden below draws the cool air up through the house.

The larger of the two internal open spaces is the garden, with a meandering trail of stepping-stones (*right*). All the rooms on the ground floor give on to this, as does a balcony above from the upper-floor living-room.

Courtyard houses had their origin in China, as this Ming merchant's dwelling in Anhui Province, but the principle was taken up and adapted to Japanese conditions (*below*).

On the other side of the living area from the balcony that overlooks the garden is the second, smaller courtyard, bounded on two sides by the outer wall of the house and open to the living, dining and kitchen areas (*left* and *below*). The larch decking is stained with persimmon juice, a traditional weathering treatment. Air circulation follows a principle of old Kyoto houses, which often had two tiny gardens, one easily warmed, the other not. The pair functioned as a generator of wind passing through interior space.

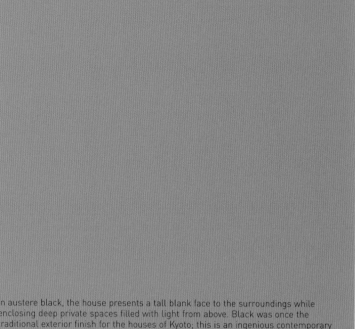

In austere black, the house presents a tall blank face to the surroundings while enclosing deep private spaces filled with light from above. Black was once the traditional exterior finish for the houses of Kyoto; this is an ingenious contemporary version of the time-honoured practice (*these pages*).

{Mobile gardens and rooms} The position of mobility and re-arrangement is inherent in the traditional Japanese manipulation of space. *Shoji* (light cedarwood frames over which is stretched handmade paper) and *fusuma* (solid panels) slide open, close and detach to alter the configuration of interior spaces and to extend interiors into adjoining gardens. Yasuhiro Harada, designer and restaurateur, takes this adaptable principle of impermanence a contemporary step further in the form of miniature mobile gardens, and then from these to a new restaurant concept. The mobile gardens are in fact trays in polished stainless steel, filled with freeze-dried moss, white and black pebbles (in the *kare-sansui* 'dry stone garden' tradition), all at different heights so that they can slide and stack partly under each other.

The idea proved so successful that Harada incorporated it into what has grown to be a chain of restaurants. The first use in 2002, at a restaurant called Sou-en, was to have them scattered and staggered at different heights in the two-storey underground space. A little later, in a restaurant in Roppongi, Tokyo, called Cube Hatago, they were combined with entire rooms on the same mobile principle. This is boom-time in the restaurant business in the big Japanese cities, and naturally highly competitive. With the quality of food and service always high, most Japanese restaurants survive or fail on what else they provide, notably ambience, original concept and surprising aesthetic experiences.

At Cube Hatago, the surprise comes in the form of a kind of re-creation of an old post-town, with private mobile dining-rooms on wheels. The anti-quated term *hatago* refers to an old-style accommodation in post-towns during the 16th-century Edo period. As in post-towns everywhere, trav-ellers broke their journey to dine and sleep. This modern version in Roppongi, one of the liveliest downtown entertainment districts of Tokyo, is a two-storey underground space that offers a modern type of stopover. Private dining spaces are traditionally rare and expensive in Japan, but here the experience, in wooden cubes that remind diners of *chashitsu* (tea-ceremony rooms), is affordable. Harada's mobile gardens feature here as floor arrangements and on the roofs of the rooms.

This interchangeable, temporary allocation of space has more recently been extended to a hugely popular rooftop restaurant in Osaka. Called Ten-Chou-En, mobile rooms and mobile garden trays sit under the sky in a bed of pebbles, accessed by a boardwalk, overlooking the city and the river. An even more temporary aspect to Ten-Chou-En is that guests 'rent' the rooms and order meals, by telephone, from a wide range of restaurants in the building below.

A set of a dozen mobile tray gardens, in different sizes and all on wheels, fill the terrace of the designer's Tokyo penthouse (*right*).

Miniaturized even further, gardens become trays in beds of white gravel to fill a small ledge in one of the intimate dining spaces in CubeZen, a restaurant in Tokyo's Aoyama district (*above*).

At Cube Hatago in Roppongi, the blacked-out surroundings add to the feeling of a post-town in the night, and the wheeled mobile rooms can be re-arranged into different configurations **(opposite)**.

Mobile gardens and individually constructed rooms fill the roof terrace of a department store overlooking the Osaka river **(left)**.

The stainless steel trays, all on wheels, are at different heights so that they can slide under and over each other **(below left)**.

No useful space is neglected. At Cube Hatago, the roof of each mobile room is itself a modern version of a dry-stone garden (originally a Zen concept) **(below)**.

{3. Materials}

Most Oriental architectural and design forms can be traced back to ways of using specific materials. These include wood of various kinds, such as teak in Burma and Thailand, cypress in Shinto buildings in Japan, bamboo for flooring, panels, furniture and countless other products, as well as being used structurally throughout south-east Asia. Other important traditional materials include ceramics for tiles, walls, floors and vessels, paper for light-transmitting screens, terracotta, stone, straw, silk and lacquer. Whether used for the fabric of a building or for its internal fixtures and fittings, materials throughout most Oriental societies have attracted a particular care and respect in the way they are worked. The skill of the craftsman is highly regarded to the point, where at its highest expression, it is considered as art. From the carved panelling of a Thai temple door, to the glaze of a celadon bowl, or the pattern of fibres in hand-moulded paper, there are endless examples of the tactile, sensual appreciation of materials.

The 20th century changed most of this, through the introduction of reinforced concrete and steel. Architect Kengo Kuma has written, 'If I were to describe the architecture of the 20th century with one word, it would be "concrete." Its freedom and universality fit the 20th century so well that other local methods of construction were abandoned.' It also helped further the idea of the house as a strong, secure little fortress, and on a larger scale encouraged a trend towards monumental structures. There are arguments, however, that modern dwellings can be lighter and less substantial, with the use of materials more in accord with the principles illustrated in the foregoing section of this book.

This is not to deny the valuable properties of concrete, which is in any case open to a variety of interesting treatments, as some of the buildings illustrated in this book show. However, there are many other possible materials both for construction and for cladding, and many Oriental architects and designers are now exploring them. As shown on the following pages, these include traditional materials such as wood and bamboo that have been treated in new ways, while others are new materials such as plastic used to interpret traditional forms.

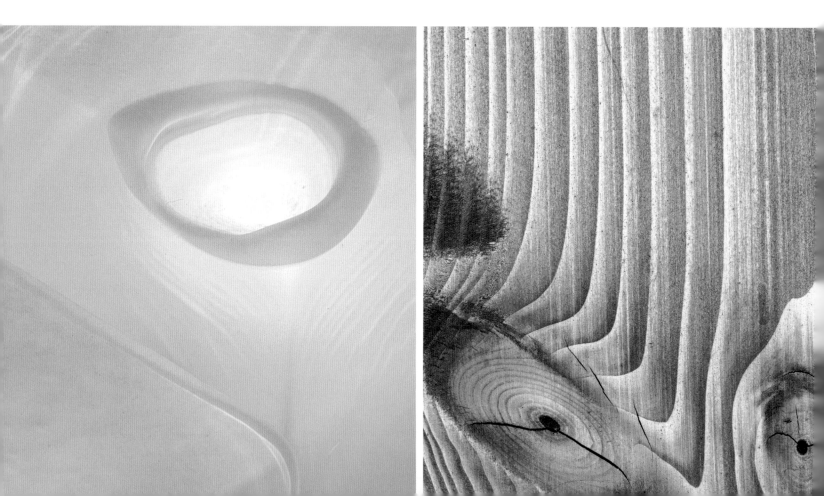

Cast glass lights by Takeshi Nagasaki carry the imprints of the stones among which they are set (*opposite left*).

Black-stained wood in the house Abode of Clouds, by Michimasa Kawaguchi (*opposite right*).

Detail of a Balinese covered bowl made in beeswax (*below left*).

Pieces of rope embedded in a handmade plaster wall, by Terunobu Fujimori (*below right*).

{Bamboo Wall House, Commune by the Shuiguan Great Wall, nr. Beijing}

The Commune by the Great Wall, completed in 2002, is an élite development of eleven houses scattered over the slopes of a small valley below a section of the Shuiguan Great Wall at its closest to Beijing. Conceived by developer Zhang Xin and her husband Pan Shiyi, it showcases modern Asian architecture — the architects are all from Asian countries. Zhang Xin believes that 'commerce is the most effective way to promote the art and architecture', and this venture aims 'to influence a whole generation of architects, developers and consumers in China'. Experimental is the keyword, within the two constraints given to the architects of using local materials and fitting the house to the topography.

One of the most successful constructions is by Japanese architect Kengo Kuma, who created a remarkable building that uses unprocessed bamboo. Hundreds of poles frame the exterior, partition spaces inside, and in the centre create an ethereal room that seems suspended in its own dimension — an open cube, sheltered by glass, over a shallow reflecting pool that looks out over the Shuiguan hills.

This was not Kuma's first experience with bamboo — he had built a seaside house in Kanagawa, Japan, in 1999, making structural use of thick bamboo from near Kyoto. The posts were filled with steel-reinforced concrete — a solution that would have horrified modernists. Here, however, he was aware of the aesthetic differences between the types of bamboo. A major consideration was 'to make the delicacy of the building conform to the delicacy of the landscape', and as it was the 'roughness' of the landscape surrounding the Great Wall that gives it its character, Kuma chose the bamboo poles used in China for scaffolding, which had the appropriate lack of delicacy. Aware that the line between a satisfying roughness and coarse vulgarity is fine, he first put up a number of full-scale models using this class of material to see how it would conform to the landscape. The Chinese workers lived up to his expectations and achieved the right balance, and between them, they created what Kuma calls 'a common perception of delicacy .... a new way of communication.'

The Shuiguan Great Wall is the part closest to Beijing, and this section overlooks the small valley (to the right of this view) that contains the Commune development and the Bamboo Wall House (right).

Rather than level the site, the undulating topography was left intact, and the slender architecture was built directly on to the slope, mirroring the Great Wall that can be seen from the house (above).

Adapting the principle of the *engawa*, the traditional Japanese form of projecting veranda, the heart of the house is a room for serving tea and for contemplation. Protected by glass on the outside, the room is defined by screens of bamboo that hang over a small moat of water that also serves as a reflecting pool (*these pages*). Rough bamboo is used throughout east and south-east Asia as scaffolding, and normally not considered for construction itself. Here, workers help to restore the golden stupa at Bangkok's Grand Palace (*above*).

The living and dining areas are encased in bamboo, from ceiling to outer wall, and the shadows cast by the winter sun add a distinctive quality of chiaroscuro to the interior (*above left*).

A bamboo screen at the end of the corridor containing the bedrooms (*above right*); the unevenness of the poles contrasts with the minimalist finish of the walls, ceiling and floor.

The architect decided 'to build an equally rough house in line with the roughness of the landscape and turn the two into a harmonious existence.' Key to this is his use of contrasting materials, such as bamboo against stone and concrete, bamboo used as shelving and for bathroom fittings, and in combination with one wall that is essentially an acrylic box filled with feathers, as an insulator. The spacing of the bamboo was an important consideration, and this imitates the density of the naturally growing plant (*these pages*).

{Furniture House, Commune by the Shuiguan Great Wall, nr. Beijing} In the same development as the previous house, another internationally-known Japanese architect, Shigeru Ban, created 'The Furniture House', so-called because of its structural invention. While its neo-Palladian form and light, open design are the most immediately striking features, the central concern was that of what material to use. Ban has been experimenting for a long time with inexpensive and accessible materials in unlikely structural uses. One of his earlier inventions was structural cardboard tubing, reinforced where necessary with concrete. Here, the part of the brief that specified local materials set him investigating local suppliers. Lumber was in short supply (wood is no longer used extensively in China), but, as he explained, 'What caught my eyes instead was a kind of plywood .... a lamination of thin strips of bamboo woven into sheets.' The normal use for this is as concrete formwork, but Ban thought that it should be possible to make this structural. His experiments confirmed that by laminating the material with a particular kind of glue, it had a structural strength between steel and timber. The beams and the framing system, which includes built-in cupboards, shelving and storage, as well as the interior and exterior surfaces, are all made of this bamboo laminate — what Ban calls his 'furniture house' modular system, which he has continued to develop.

The wide span of the vaulting, ample window space, white finish and the bamboo laminate wall at the end all contribute a sense of lightness to the house.

The architect's invention of a bamboo laminate structure as demonstrated in The Furniture House is intended to have wider application. His 'furniture house' system, in which most of the items of furniture and the walls are integral to the structure, is the culmination of a 'prefabricated, modularized building system' which he has been developing for some years. Here it was used for the unit framing and beams, and for the interior and exterior finish of the walls (**above**) and in detail (**opposite**). From the dining-room (**opposite below left**) there are views of the Great Wall, while the bedroom on the opposite side (**opposite above right**) looks out over the valley.

{Abode of Clouds, Tokyo} Tokyo-based architect Michimasa Kawaguchi has established a firm reputation for designing houses that appeal to the Japanese taste for tactile natural materials. He has revived some traditional techniques while adapting and combining others, such as using different concentrations of calligraphy ink to stain timber and applying crumpled hand-moulded paper to wall surfaces. In this house, completed in 2005, Kawaguchi added a new dimension — a skywards progression of materials from dense to light, so that it moves conceptually from basement to eaves. Its fitting name translates approximately as 'Abode of Clouds'.

Including the basement level, which is open at one end via a light-well and steps leading up to the small garden, there are four storeys. On each of these, two structural materials dominate. The basement combines stone floor, concrete walls and ceiling cast with wood planking for the formwork. The ground floor is concrete and ink-stained timber, but here the concrete is treated quite differently, with a hand-chiselled, strongly textured finish. Up one floor, timber and a straw-flecked earthen plaster take over. Finally, on the top floor, the timber, including an undressed tree trunk supporting one of the asymmetrical roof ridges, is combined with *washi* paper. Thus, each floor has its own character, strongly tactile, yet is linked by its texture with the next.

The most massive materials are used for the lowest level — the basement (*right*). The floor is laid with diagonally aligned old Chinese stone bricks, with walls and ceiling of concrete. The ceiling pattern is that of the timber formwork, while the walls are hand-finished in the style shown overleaf for the ground floor.

Concrete and wood are the materials for the ground floor. The roughened concrete finish (*opposite*) is known as *hatsuri*, and the hammering by hand to achieve this effect was a communal effort by family members and friends over a period of seven months. The vestibule with a niche is circular (*opposite below left*) and inside solid wooden screens can divide the floor as needed (*opposite above right*). A small study is located in the corner by the stairs (*left*). The entrance path curves around a tiny strip garden to the door. The exterior finish is in black-stained timber planking (*above*).

A two-tiered counter in Japanese oak zig-zags across the first floor (US: second), where the dominant materials have become lighter (*left*) — stained wood and walls of a rough earthen render with pieces of straw. A dumb-waiter elevator carries dishes from the kitchen here to the basement dining-room.

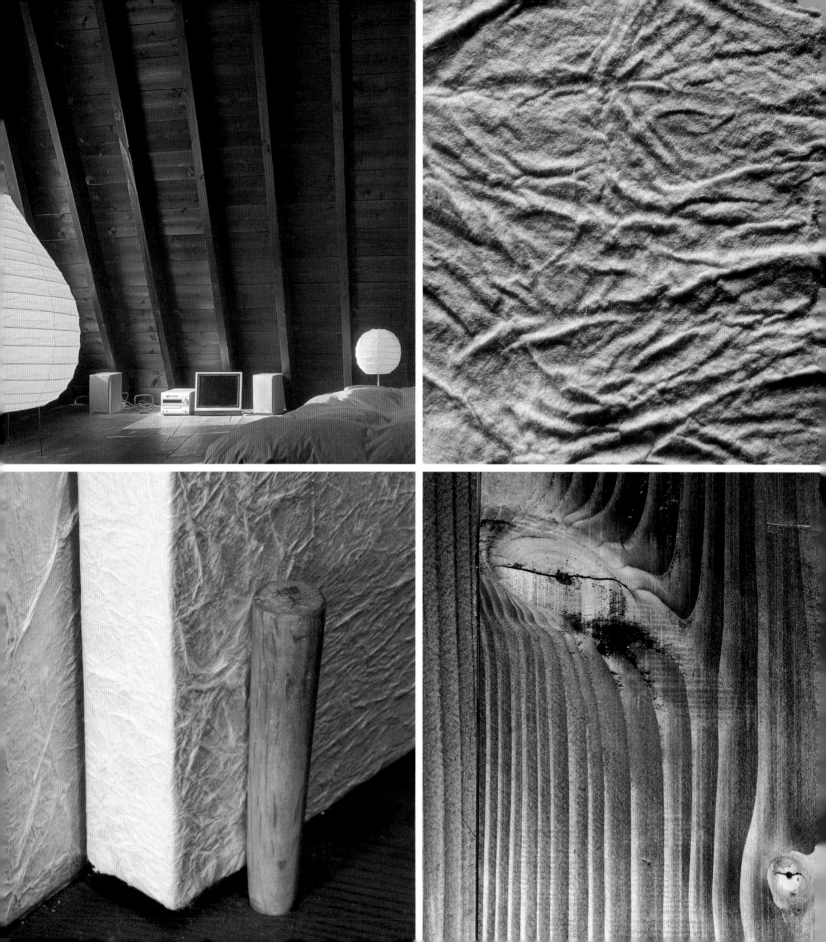

The top floor, with the bedroom (*opposite above left*) and bathroom, is under the eaves, and here the materials are the lightest combination of all — the same ink-stained timber as on the floor below and *washi*, hand-laid Japanese paper. Some of the timbers, however, are undressed logs (*above*), and Kawaguchi's treatment of the paper is to lay it rough and crinkled on interior dividers and the door. A simple wooden peg (*opposite below left*), serves as a door-stop.

{Hardy House, Bali} The owners of this house overlooking the Sayam Terraces near Ubud, Bali, wanted a construction that was both 'transparent' and with minimal impact on the site. Silver designer John Hardy and his wife Cynthia acquired the land overlooking the deeply incised Ayung river for its spectacular view and began by living on the site in a tent. Both 'nature lovers with a fantasy about living in trees', the Hardys wanted the setting and view to define the house. They approached Malaysian architect Cheong Yew Kuan, and began a long process of experimentation. Cheong's sense of materials and the clients' insistence on a naturalistic treatment informed the process. At the start of the project, in 1993, they acquired a few hundred square-sectioned ironwood poles, some of the thousands that had been used as electricity poles across the island and were being auctioned off as the government replaced them with concrete. Each was twenty feet long.

The ironwood made it possible to construct a form that was inspired by the Iban long-houses of central Borneo. As the name implies, these structures, raised high above the forest floor, are long enough to accommodate an entire community of up to 70 families. The longest reach 260 metres. For the Hardys' house, this long elevated structure achieved three ideals. First, it put the dwelling among the trees. It also functions as a wide balcony for maximum exposure to the spectacular view. Lastly, the space below remains open to the view beyond, so that on entering the property through the walled gate, the first thing the visitor notices is the rice terracing across the valley rather than the house. A love of materials and their possibilities on the part of both architect and client is evident throughout. In addition to the ironwood beams there are sections of tree-trunks, bamboo strips woven into wall panels, mud walls, pebbles, rough tiles and wood in every conceivable form, from undressed branches to rough slabs.

A raised walkway connects the upper living-room with the bedroom, looking down on to the plunge pool and across the valley to the Sayam rice terraces (*right*).

Inspiration for the long structure, with its tree-level views, came from traditional Iban long-houses, such as this one in Borneo on a tributary of the Rajah river (*below*).

Hardy himself made his bed out of pieces of teak and antique ironwood. The mosquito netting was made from the material used to strain tofu (*opposite above left*). An upstairs wall made from a thick weave of bamboo strips, painted yellow (*opposite above right*). The washbasin in copper and brass uses the hammered finish that identifies much of Hardy's silver jewelry design (*opposite below left*). A small seating area at one end of the ground floor, using the woven bamboo panels shown in detail above; the print is by local photographer Rio Helmi (*opposite below right*). Knowing that the client, as a jeweller, enjoys playing with texture and materials, the architect followed this as much as possible by using a huge variety of natural materials, from the stone of the water basin in the foreground, to adobe, river pebbles, ironwood poles and rough-hewn wooden slabs. Living, dining and cooking is at ground-level, although the complete openness makes the description 'rooms' redundant (*right*).

A recent addition to the house is this tiered guest-bedroom structure, set over a small pond and air-conditioned. The design of diminishing thatched tiers was inspired by the *merus* of Balinese temples (*below*).

The view from the adobe return of the open central staircase (*right*), looking over a giant quartz crytal to the *bale* thatched pavilion; the roof, supported by *balam* wooden poles, is made of fibreglass-coated muslin.

The long span of the house, with its obvious references to Borneo long-houses, is best appreciated from the valley side of the property (*above* and *opposite above right* and *below left*). A plunge pool is built of local stone. A Y-shaped tree trunk has been cut into a table for the living area (*opposite above left*), and a row of wooden rice containers stands in front of the seating (*opposite below right*).

{Izumi House, Shikoku} In a corner of the most famous stonemason's yard in Japan, this granite house was designed and built by its owner, Masatoshi Izumi, in spare moments over the period of a year. Takamatsu on the island of Shikoku was home for many years to the sculptor Isamu Noguchi, who was buried here in the small settlement near the foot of the granite hills that produce the famous Aji stone. When Noguchi died, his workshop became a museum. Born into a family of stone-carvers, Izumi was Noguchi's close collaborator for two decades until the latter's death, co-founding the Stone Atelier and developed a studio complex here.

For this highly personal project, Izumi took time in selecting the right stones, varying the size for dynamic effect. The flooring is constructed from recycled paving stones that originally carried tram tracks in the city of Osaka, and the roof structure consists of exposed steel trusses. Paper *shoji* screens and the Akari paper lanterns designed by Noguchi provide contrasts of texture and mass. The interior spaces, too, have great variety, from a spacious open-plan living area to an independent circular stone room, and a meditation space.

The stoneworks scattered about the entrance of the house are a reminder that this is an extension of a sculptor's atelier and stonemason's yard (*below*).

A room created by Izumi for contemplation, with *tatami* floor and *shoji* screens, features a massive granite wall, each stone handpicked (*right*).

The Aji granite that makes this area of Shikoku island famous is used in a number of forms. The floor is of old paving stones once used for an Osaka tram track, while the walls are made of stones direct from the local quarry. Izumi chose them slowly in his spare time, and the variety of sizes gives a dynamic feeling to the space. A sculpture sits below one of his partner Noguchi's paper lantern designs (*overleaf*).

{Gentry House, Bali} Overlooking the Sayam Terraces, Ubud, architect Cheong Yew Kuan had another commission, this time for a second house for a Hong Kong-based training consultant. Like his other design there (an appreciation of the view driving much of the design) Cheong indulged his love of natural materials, but the overall solution is quite unique, as it needed to resolve two potentially conflicting client demands — for rusticity, yet also for a refined formality.

The approach to the house is through a modest gate in a side wall of the track leading down from a lane, the first step in a slow process of revealing the beauty of the house and its view. From the gate, a gently winding path leads along a small lake, from the end of which stepping-stones lead across to the entrance of the main building. This is actually more a built-in pavilion or gatehouse, in adobe and timber with benches on each side and narrow steps leading up to a small perch. The immediate view is of a huge boulder surrounded by water. Continuing through, the visitor emerges on to a veranda with an expanded view over a large reflecting pool towards the terraces and forest on the opposite, western side of the valley. This second water body is the heart of the dwelling. The living area opens out on to it, with the master bedroom wing on the left and a separated office on the right. A wooden deck extends from the veranda, cut back to enclose the boulder, giving it an uncanny resemblance to the view from the Asian Gate House in Okinawa.

To one side, a wing containing the master bedroom projects out over the slope, its deck supported by long wooden posts.

The contrast of textures reflects the combination of tastes of the owners, one of whom likes rough and natural finishes, the other preferring a more polished finish. The table (*opposite above right*) is a simply dressed block of rainforest hardwood half a metre thick, while natural splits in the metre-wide floor planking of local *merbau* hardwood (*Intsia sp.*) are held with butterfly joints (*opposite below right*). The 12-ton boulder that dominates the pool (*opposite below left*) had to be brought in by crane. In contrast is the guest accommodation one level below the main house, built into the steep hillside (*opposite above left* and *above*) in polished and sculpted concrete and curved timber.

Reflected on the other side of the lake at sunset are the main and adjoining buildings, from the kitchen at the extreme left to the separate study on the right. The entrance path curves around the 4-metre-deep lake (*left*).

Perched at the edge of the steep slope that drops away below the house and pool is a *bale*, a Balinese-style pavilion, used for evening drinks and admiring the view over the terraces (*above*).

{Miyashita Restaurant, Tokyo} Located in a fashionable part of Tokyo, Gaien-mae, midway between Omote-sando and Shibuya, Miyashita is a small, upmarket restaurant serving Japanese cuisine. Architect Kengo Kuma, whose offices are directly above in this new building, conceived a minimal, restrained design that combined traditional and modern materials.

The traditional material that he chose is the handmade paper known as *washi*, but employed in a non-traditional way. Normally used as a translucent screen in sliding *shoji* screens, in Miyashita it is a wall covering. This demanded a solution to the problem of scuffing. *Washi* is normally never put in a position where it needs to be touched, but in a small dining-room people would inevitably lean on the walls. However, the architect had worked intensively with *washi* before, designing a community meeting-house for a town in Niigata prefecture famous for its hand-moulded paper. There he had decided to make the exterior walls from the paper, and had been introduced to a protective treatment by a local *washi* craftsman, Yasuo Kobayashi. This consisted of coating the paper with a liquid made by mashing bulbs of the *konnyaku* plant and another liquid, called *kakishibu*, made from fermented unripe persimmons. This was used for the walls of Miyashita, on paper from the same craftsmen in Niigata. The technique, incidentally, was used rather oddly at the end of the Second World War for 40,000 paper 'balloon bombs' launched across the Pacific to the United States (600 made landfall and caused six deaths).

Kuma's sensual approach to materials, reinforced by whatever research and development is necessary to bring out their tactile qualities fully, suggests a modern *sukiya* style of restraint and intense attention to detail. With handmade *washi* paper figuring so prominently in the building, it would be surprising if there were not some reference to the *shoji* screens that traditionally slide along wooden grooves and are lightweight, translucent, removable dividers. Here, however, the reference is unexpected and subtle. The interior walls are transparent acrylic panels covered with paper on both sides. In the evening, depending on the balance of lighting between rooms and corridors, an almost imperceptible glow emanates from the walls.

Formal simplicity in one of the private dining-rooms, with a cherrywood table against the paper-covered wall; paper is also used for the floor cushions and covers the acrylic wall at right.

Strands of black bamboo line the path leading up to the entrance, parallel to the façade of the building, and also act as a screen for the privacy of diners (*below*). Just in front of the door is a miniature garden of two mounds of moss on white gravel (*left*).

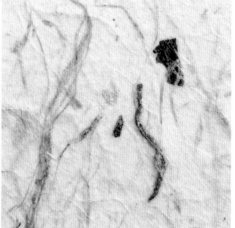

Paper-covered acrylic walls float over thin illuminated troughs (*left*), so that the internal reflections in the acrylic sheets can be seen along their edges (similar in principle to fibre-optics). Fibre-optics in the ceiling cast precise pools of light on the table. The lighting design is by Shozo Toyohisa. A detail of the *washi* used for the wall-covering (*above*); in close-up, the distinctive character of each paper becomes apparent. This example was made by one papermaker, Yasuo Kobayashi of Echigo Kadode Washi in the town of Takayanagi. At the sushi counter, a maple leaf inlay subtly decorates one place setting (*opposite above right*). On an *urushi* black lacquer tray, wooden chopsticks rest on a porcelain holder (*opposite below left*). A simple asymmetrical flower arrangement enlivens a flat black ceramic vase (*opposite below right*). Formal wall decoration creates a point of focus above the table (*opposite above left*).

{House in Pattaya, Gulf of Thailand} On Thailand's eastern seaboard, the site for this holiday home on the gentle slope of a low range of hills was carefully chosen for its wide view over the coast. The approach here was to create a modern version of the *reuan thai*, the traditional form of a number of units linked by platforms and terraces. To this end, wood was to be used extensively; a tiled roof would have the traditional function of sheltering the verandas with a deep overhang, and there would be the same unity of indoor and outdoor spaces — but all without mimicry or pastiche.

The design of the roof in particular was the subject of careful thought by the architects, A49. Simply transposing the distinctive Thai-style roof on to a modern structure has become a cliché of hotel, restaurant and villa design in Thailand. Even despite its questionable taste, the exercise is frequently non-functional. The steep pitch of a traditional Thai roof works on small domestic units, and in a grander way on long halls and palace buildings, but would look ridiculous on the spacious two-storey main building here. Nor was its heat-extraction function necessary, as shutters and sliding glass panels were designed to open both floors completely on three sides for ventilation. The pitch of the two tiers, therefore, could be made much shallower. A deep projecting overhang had to be maintained, however, for shade, and called for a version of the distinctively Thai structural device, the eave bracket. Called a *nakkatan*, it supports the relatively heavy eaves from the posts, and has its own lore, traditions and regional variations.

For the most part wood prevails — in the post-and-beam structure, for shutters and many of the walls, and for the extensive decking that connects the buildings around the pool. The sliding doors that can open fully are based on the traditional *ban fiam*, or Chinese-door style.

Carved eave brackets are a distinctive feature of traditional Thai building, here in the highly stylized shape of *naga* serpents on the house of the former Governor of Lampang (*above*).

A projection of the roof all around, supported by eave brackets, is an important element in Thai construction, essential for comfort in this tropical climate. Integrated with the post-and-beam construction, these modern brackets fulfil the same function as the more decorative *nakkatan* illustrated on the previous page. Where necessary, steel beams have been introduced for structural lightness and efficiency (*opposite*). The dining-room has a carefully framed view of the lush sub-tropical vegetation outside (*above*).

{Pine Tree House, Hakata} Terunobu Fujimori, architect and professor at Tokyo University, has for many years followed an idiosyncratic course, somewhere between eco-architecture, historical research and a modern Japanese version of Arts and Crafts. In all his projects, wood and other natural materials play a leading role, and where metal must be used he favours hand-beaten copper. All of this is directed towards a greening of the urban environment, in contrast to what he calls the 'White School' of metal-and-glass architecture.

Many of his buildings look for a kind of symbiosis between nature and dwelling, so that, 'the building and the flowers are unified, or rather combined, in such a way that they support each other's character.' In the city of Hakata, on the southern island of Kyushu, he designed and built (crafted may be a better expression) the Pine Tree House, named perfectly obviously for its commanding feature, a pine tree planted at its apex. The design began with a square plan and a steeply pitched pyramidal roof, and Fujimori knew from the start that he wanted something growing on this. Having already incorporated plantings into roofs in his own house and in one for a painter friend, he was familiar with the technical demands. He first thought of grass, in the manner of *shibamune*, the old earth-and-grass-roofed dwellings now long gone from rural Japan, but rejected this as being too soft for the vigorous roof-line. He decided that a 'symbolic form' was necessary. The client was moving from an old family mansion in a traditional style, and at first he was a little nervous about her reaction. As it turned out, she was delighted at having her house crowned with what looked like 'a samurai's top-knot', as she described it.

In an idiosyncratic attempt at greening the urban environment, a single pine tree occupies pride of place at the apex of the copper-clad roof (all hand-beaten) (*right*). It also receives the full attention of a *bonsai* expert once a year to keep its growth and shapeliness under control (*below*). A concealed stainless-steel trough holds the soil and moisture.

Detailing throughout receives architect Fujimori's highly personal touch, with extensive use of wood, often in its natural shape. One invention used in the bedroom (*opposite*) and in the living-room is a lamp in the form of a globe suspended in netting from a branch. This rises into the open space formed by the pyramidal roof. Other rustic details include a roughly hollowed-out water-spout in wood (*left*), a miniature reprise of the main roof over the entrance gate, capped with copper (*below left*), and wooden pegging to secure a bracket to the exterior wooden wall (*below*).

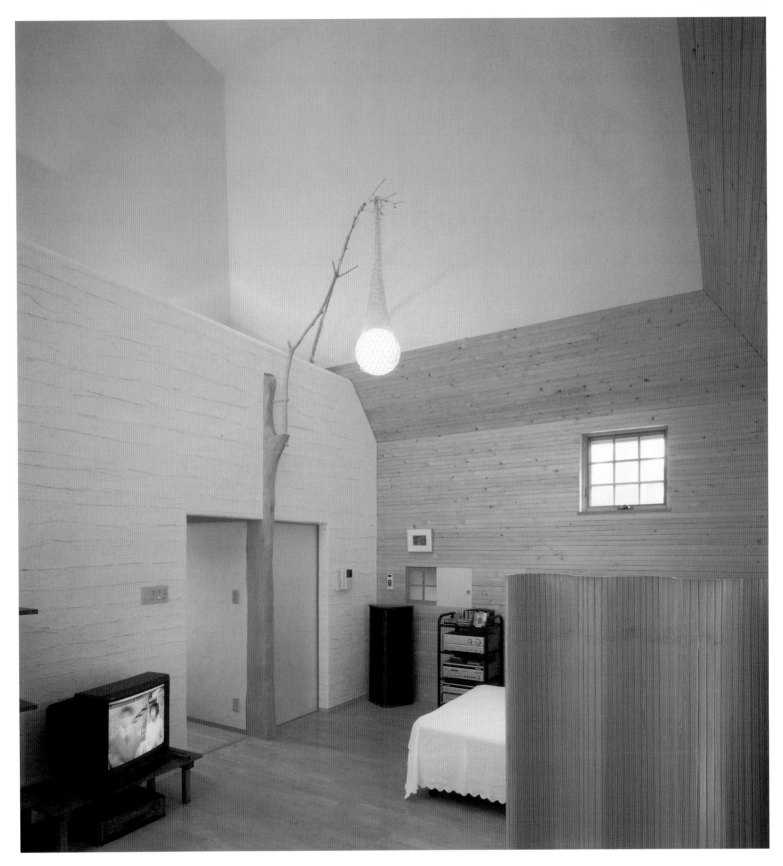

{Plastic House, Tokyo} Not only are old materials being put to uncommon and oblique uses by the present generation of Japanese architects and designers, but new materials are also being given a traditional interpretation. In Meguro, an old-established residential neighbourhood in central Tokyo, Kengo Kuma designed in 2002 a house for a photographer and his mother, a writer, using fibreglass-reinforced plastic (FRP). Kuma's search for 'weak' structures, plus a fondness for surprise, led him to this unlikely material. The walls are a laminate of FRP sandwiching translucent thermal insulation sheeting; at the back of the house, a platform and exterior walls are constructed from thin FRP beams.

Traditional Japanese *sukiya*-style architecture involved, as part of its modesty and lightness, the use of carefully chosen and crafted materials. These included wood, paper, bamboo and various earthen renders incorporating straw and other particles. In the Plastic House, FRP is given the same kind of attention. According to the quality of the enclosed fibres, it can have the appearance of rice paper, and sometimes of bamboo, enhanced by its milky-green colour. What the architect calls its 'biotic softness and tenderness' makes it a modern/traditional material, which suited the photographer client who wanted a space with 'simple' rather than 'decorative' beauty.

The open-plan ground floor functions as living-room, kitchen and dining area, meeting room and even photographic studio when needed. Bedrooms and bathroom are on the upper floor, and the entire roof is a terrace. The photographer's mother has the basement level as an independent apartment.

The rooftop, with its box-like plastic access, functions as an open-air studio and a party space, overlooking Meguro's residential skyline (*right*); the door is covered with FRP grating (*below*).

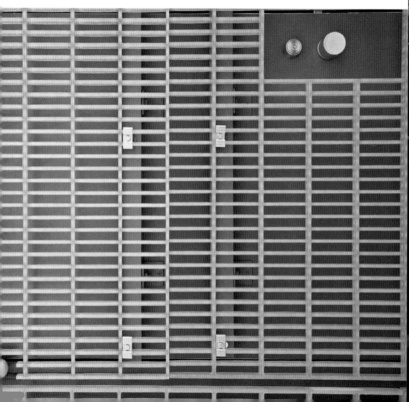

The exterior of the house changes appearance due to the softness of the material — at the same time synthetic yet organic. The walls are laminates of a translucent insulating material between 4 mm FRP sheets, which themselves have a translucent milkiness; the effect intentionally recalls traditional light-transmitting *shoji* sliding screens (*left*).
At night, the house glows like a lantern (*opposite*). The prominent box-like projection from the master bedroom (*above*) is both a small terrace and a frame for the view, on clear days, of Mount Fuji.

At the rear of the house (*left* and *below*), a platform of FRP beams raised over the white gravel surface of the garden serves the same function as would *tatami* mats in a traditional interior. Kuma prizes the organic quality of the material, which is weathering green with age. By using plastic screws and fittings, he is acknowledging the Japanese artisan technology in which a single material gives coherent character. The ground-floor room can serve as studio, living or dining area.

{Modern teak villas, Mae Rim, nr. Chiang Mai} The history of Thai architecture is inextricably bound up with one material — teak. Most of the wood came from the northern forests of Lanna, and in the 19th century there were upwards of 4,000 elephants employed in logging and transporting. Production reached its peak when the British were given concessions in the 19th century (as a commercial appeasement to deal with the political threat of encroachment) and brought with them Burmese workers and merchants. Over-cutting more recently, however, has led to a complete ban on teak logging, and while there are now plantations, the tree grows slowly, and teak wood is hard to come by.

A cluster of weekend villas near the small town of Mae Rim, a little way north of Chiang Mai in the lee of Doi Suthep and its neighbouring hills, was designed for different clients, but with a common theme of teak used in a northern Thai way. The vernacular forms adapted for these small holiday homes included shingled roofs made of the local small wooden tiles, plastered brick, terracotta tiles, and the distinctive superstructures. These last are a 19th-century import from northern Burma; as a result of the British teak logging of the period, there remain scattered throughout the north a number of Shan-style monasteries, built by and for the Shans that came with them. The most characteristic element of these monasteries, which are usually single buildings, is the diminishing multi-tiered roof.

The three houses illustrated here combine all of the above. Baan Kamonorrathep, the first to be built, features a hipped roof, though much shallower than a traditional one, with three diminishing tiers above. A pool occupies the heart of the site, and the house faces across this to the small *sala*, or open pavilion. The neighbouring Baan Penjati, is raised on pillars in the traditional Thai style, and its *sala* is reached by an elevated walkway from a wooden veranda. Baan Rimtai, built for an elderly client and so all on one level, makes use of the extra available height to expose the wooden ceiling and the interior of the roof superstructure.

One of the purest surviving Shan monastery complexes is Wat Chom Sawan, built between 1910 and 1912 in Phrae, also in northern Thailand (*above*). Its interlocking buildings feature a variety of superimposed roofs.

Seen from across the pool in the late afternoon, Baan Kamonorrathep displays an adaptation of the typical Shan hipped roof topped by a small superstructure, itself with a steeply pitched roof (*right*). This is actually a false storey designed for heat extraction; windows and gaps in the upper wall draw hot air upwards for a gently cooling breeze.

A broad staircase rises to Baan Penjati from the entrance gate (*opposite*), after a narrow pond lined with urns. The balustrade at right is a streamlined version of the traditional *naga-makara* style, featuring a serpent's body rearing up at the base; this came originally from Khmer temples in Cambodia.

The superimposed roof tiers of Baan Kamonorrathep (*left*), the lower three hipped and the top gabled.

The interior of Baan Rimtai makes use of the high space below its tiered roofs as a light-well, supplemented by concealed artificial lighting (*below left*).

A wooden bridge raised high above the ground (*below*) connects the main building of Baan Penjati to a small pavilion for relaxing, known as a *sala*.

{4. Essence}

There is a massive and vibrant Asian influence in the Western love of minimalism. The word 'minimalism' has probably been over-used to the point where it implies a certain geometrical austerity and modernity. Both of these qualities are possible, but neither is a necessary qualification, and in looking back over the history of dwellings and lifestyles across Asia we can see pure minimalism in many traditional forms. In the east Asian sphere, the refinements of Ming Dynasty Chinese design (for example, furniture, and the cubic white merchants' dwellings of Anhui) were highly influential. They were translated and adapted in particular ways in Korea and in Japan, which cultures created their own distinctive forms. In Japan this influence was overlaid on a sense of structural simplicity inherited from the design of Shinto shrines and the conceptual simplicity of the *chashitsu* — the small rooms used for the Way of Tea (of which new exciting versions are being created by modern architects and designers). In south-east Asia we can see something akin to Shinto simplicity in vernacular forms, in which a simple regard for the intrinsic qualities of materials frequently produced a natural, unsophisticated minimalism.

In a broader sense, we are dealing here with a reduction to essentials, which can be philosophical as well as visual. Finding and expressing the essential in design has a new urgency, as rapid change affects the major cities, and as information technologies make an ever stronger impact on lifestyles. In the contemporary city, there is a blurring of distinctions between spaces, increasing urban fragmentation and a re-evaluation of homes as centres of stability and permanence. This is happening elsewhere in the world also, but Asian cities like Tokyo, Shanghai and Seoul start with a possible cultural advantage. We should not forget that almost all traditional Oriental philosophies, including Buddhism, interpreted reality, according to architectural historian Botond Bognar, 'as a non-dual condition in which all distinctions merge. Accordingly, imagination, dreams, and all intangible phenomena are also part of our perceived reality.'

Handrail inset into a wall leading down from the gallery at Art Space N, near Tokyo (*opposite left*).

A niche bookshelf designed for a single volume, at the Tofu House, Kyoto (*opposite right*).

Detail of an interior wall at Higashi-ya, in Naka-Meguro (*below left*).

Curved wall of woven bamboo strips at Kapal Bambu in Bali (*below right*).

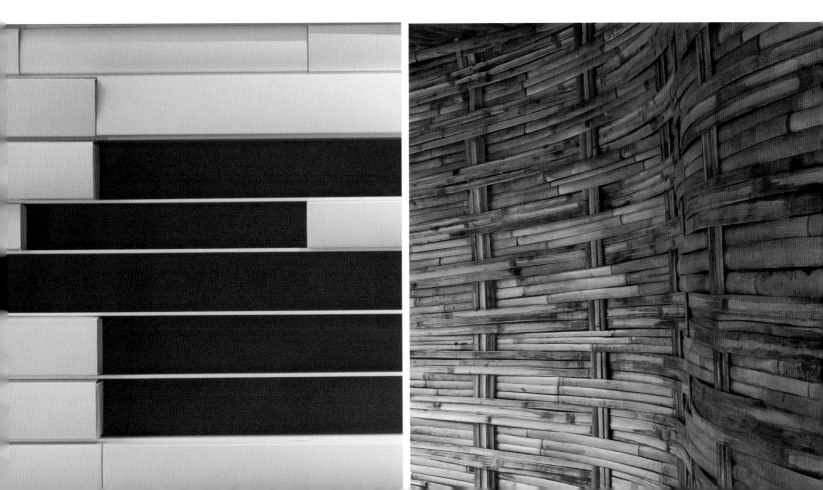

{Metal Office, nr. Kyoto and Osaka} For the new headquarters of Dynamic Tools Corporation, a precision engineering company located in a new academic research town close to Kyoto and Osaka, the client wanted a space that would not only reflect the corporate image, but would actually contribute to the research work being carried out there — would, in other words, create an environment that would put employees and visitors in an appropriate frame of mind. The architectural practice Takashi Yamaguchi and Associates, already well-known for their strikingly modernist Glass Temple and White Temple in Kyoto, were commissioned; they produced a design that is severely minimalist and completely inorganic.

In keeping with the nature of the company's work, Yamaguchi chose metal as the dominant material. Metal panels — a combination of of 5 mm aluminium laminate and galvanized steel — cover not only interior and exterior walls, but also the ceilings, while the floors are polished aluminium plates. Together with floor-to-ceiling windows, those on the ground floor sandblasted, the effect is a remarkable atmosphere of clean, blank precision — a perfect analogy for the company's engineering research. The completely uncluttered spaces demand a rigorous approach to tidiness, but that accords with the company's ethos. It is also worth noting that only in Japan would polished metal flooring be thinkable, as naturally all shoes are removed at the entrance. Yamaguchi also built into the design a subtle manipulation of visitors' frame of mind, by creating a sequence of bright-dark-light from entrance to staircase to upper rooms, intended to produce a calming, meditative effect.

The president's office (*right*) combines walls of frosted glass (behind the desk and left) and metal in cool, neutral colours, lit by natural light and concealed uplighters so that the textures merge.

The exterior of the office building (*below*), part of a new technology and research development; the ground-floor entrance is encased in frosted glass.

The president's office (*opposite*) seen softly blurred from the meeting room; the use of glass dividers to complement the aluminium walls is designed to achieve a balance between privacy and a communal working environment.

The frosted glass around the meeting area (*above*) softly diffuses light and adds its own greenish tinge.

The darkness at the head of the stairs (*below*) is part of the architect's intention to 'connect spaces by light and dark, opening and closure, continuity and discontinuity'.

After the deeply subdued lighting of the upper-floor corridor, the door opens on to a calm grey meeting and work space, with full-height windows front and back (*right*).

Blinds over the full-height windows of the meeting room (*left*) can be adjusted to frame the view of the bamboo grove outside. The 19mm-thick glass excludes all exterior sound.

From the bright entrance, with its façade completely enclosed in translucent glass, the visitor enters the stairwell (*below*) and ascends into the darkness of the landing above.

{Kapal Bambu, Bali} Rising from a tier of rice terraces in the centre of Bali, this elegant, swooping structure looks like an evolved, unadorned version of some lost indigenous architecture from a distant island in the archipelago; but it is, remarkably, a jewelry showroom. The surroundings are no less unusual in their way, for this area of foothills south of Ubud is the rustic but highly productive workshop for an international jewelry company, that of John Hardy, a committed environmentalist. The entire complex of mud-plastered bamboo and thatch buildings, providing space for six hundred craftsmen and other workers, is secreted in the rural landscape. The property is also an organic farm, and the terrace on which this new structure, the Kapal Bambu or 'Bamboo Boat', stands is also used for growing rice.

Hardy asked Malaysian architect Cheong Yew Kuan, who earlier built the Hardys' own house nearer Ubud (see p.168), to design the showroom, 'This is a building without drawings. It started with Yew Kuan cupping his hands and then me going high into the mountains where the biggest, tallest bamboo grows.' The structure, 13 metres tall at its highest point in the middle, consists essentially of two walls of bamboo framework, thatched with local *alang alang* grass, that converge to form an undulating ridge with prow-like projections at each end and a swelling hump in the middle. The floor, and the long approach ramp across the rice terraces, is made of thick bamboo poles lashed together with sugar-palm twine. By following the dimensions and natural inclination of bamboo, the building has a simplicity and purity that is both structural and aesthetic.

The light structure holds another surprise. As a showroom it needs both a secure vault and offices. These are underground, built into the rice terrace and accessed by a bamboo staircase from within. The problem of moisture-proofing these underground rooms was solved, unusually, by rendering all the interior surfaces with local beeswax.

One of the gallery/office rooms downstairs is built into a working rice terrace. The curved wall uses a thick weave of bamboo strips. The table base is a solid log of hardwood, and the two stools are of solid beeswax, which is also used as a rendering for walls.

Seen from just below the terrace, where a young crop of rice is growing, the sharp peak above the entrance resembles the prow of a boat (*opposite*) — hence the name 'Bamboo Boat'. The spine is covered with treated translucent cotton at the top for weather protection.

Inside, the showroom, entirely in bamboo from floor to ceiling, resembles a giant nave. The two walls are separated at the ridge to allow light to stream down (*above*).

One of the underground showrooms has a display on inverted cut palm trunks (*opposite above left*); the walls are rendered in beeswax. Netting surrounds the open bathroom, where a group of parakeets perch (*opposite above right*). A close-up detail of the beeswax render (*left*); this gives a natural and fragrant waterproofing to the basement space. A washstand in the bathroom (*opposite below left*); this gives on to the side of the terraces. Plantings around the curved perimeter give privacy. In the vault, beeswax is applied over broad strips of bamboo plaited together (*opposite below right*), in the same style used in the Hardy House (*p. 170*). Plinths set in the rice terrace (*left below*) give structural support for the long bamboo poles, lashed together with black twine from sugar palms. An obliquely cut culm of bamboo forms an uplighter. At the top end of the showroom, where a bamboo path leads up the hill, a bamboo spout pours water into a stone basin (*below*).

{Tofu House, Kyoto} Named for its minimalist white cubic exterior, elevated slightly above ground-level to give it a floating appearance, the Tofu House in Kyoto is architect Jun Tamaki's expression of what he calls an 'inverted space'. The brief called for a barrier-free interior that acknowledged the needs of an elderly couple who would be leaving behind a relatively large but no longer practicable house. Thus, all had to be on one floor, and with easy access. Tamaki took this requirement as an opportunity for simplifying living space to its essentials rather than as a restriction. The overall dimensions, 8 x 14 metres, are small, but by giving it a 3.6-metre ceiling height and by organizing the core of the space so that it is completely open yet can be partitioned easily into three sections, he created a spacious and even monolithic impression.

The inversion that Tamaki refers to, and which gives the Tofu House its special character, is the sense of an interior space that has been carved out of a single white block. This impression is achieved by the use of unusually thick walls which are continually brought to the attention by a succession of deep window bays and recesses. As the architect describes it, the space is 'revealed through a process of excavation and extraction. By removing a negative void from a solid mass .... the result is a positive space'. He cites as another example the Chinese 'cave' dwellings known as *yaodong*, excavated from the loess plateau of the north.

The exterior presents a clean, sculpted block, with one window in the façade, demonstrating the massive thickness of the walls. At the same time, the building is given a lightness by the undercutting of the base (lit at night) and the apparently floating roof (*these pages*).

Tamaki's minimalist exterior echoes the white, cubic appearance of Ming dynasty merchants' homes in China's Anhui Province, which were also designed for privacy (*below*).

The central space, with what the architect calls a 'mysterious' three-and-a-half metre ceiling, is used for living, eating and sleeping, and here is shown opened completely (*opposite*). The two wooden beams, foreground and background, carry sliding doors — modern versions of traditional *fusuma* — that can disappear completely into the walls. The various recesses play an important role in defining the volume (*above*). The architect says, 'A space is always imminent within a volume. This hidden space may be revealed through a process of excavation and extraction.'

A game of *go* is in progress in one of the larger recesses, a raised seating area floored with *tatami* mats **(left)**. The dense wall wrapping the central space in fact contains kitchen, toilet, bathroom and storage spaces.

Some of the client's favourite possessions also have recesses created specifically for them — in this case, a first edition of a book on the painter Matisse in a one-volume bookcase **(below)**.

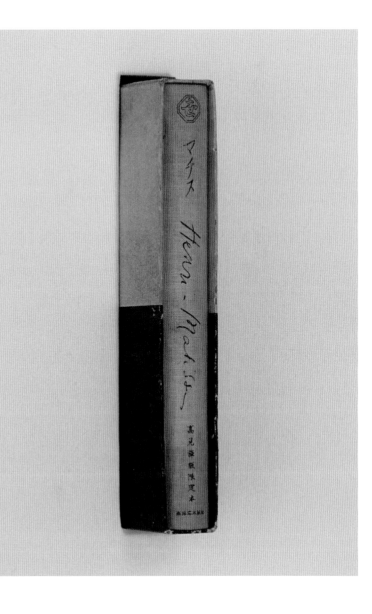

{House in Bunkyoku, Tokyo} Modernism often implies lightness and brightness in its interiors, to the point where it is largely unquestioned that 'light and airy' is an ideal. There are other cultural tastes, however, and traditional Japanese interiors are filled with the sensuality of darkness. The eminent Japanese novelist Junichiro Tanizaki, writing in 1933, at a time when Western influences were everywhere making themselves felt, extolled the virtues of dark interiors in his essay *In Praise of Shadows*. Developing the premise that 'our ancestors, forced to live in dark rooms, presently came to discover beauty in shadows', he wrote, 'I marvel at our comprehension of the secrets of shadows, our sensitive use of shadow and light', and, 'We do our walls in neutral colours so that the sad, dying rays can sink into absolute repose.'

Michimasa Kawaguchi designed this house in central Tokyo with just such a subdued, restful atmosphere in mind. The site backs on to a steep wooded hillside on temple grounds, so that the topography itself restricts access to light. Kawaguchi added to this natural effect by erecting a 5-metre-high black wooden fence. The entire house is bathed in gentle, reflected light. The choice of materials and textures inside was made for softness and coolness, with most of the walls in grey unpainted concrete, and the wooden flooring stained with calligraphy ink (*sumi*). Other interior surfaces that express the Japanese tactile sensibility are covered in *washi* paper or in plaster that has been whisked into a froth before being applied. Kawaguchi paid great attention to the views through the various windows, to avoid as much as possible direct views of the sky. The largest window, in the living-room, faces the wall of maple trees on the hillside, while others look out on to small courtyards and light-wells and, where necessary, were positioned low to control the view and the light. Because the interior surfaces are grey or black, there are few reflections in the glass when looking out.

From the living-room floor, the view out on to a small, two storey-deep courtyard is through a window sited low, so that the framing excludes the sky. Throughout the house, the architect has aimed at a gentle and shadowed atmosphere that avoids any harsh light.

Two concurrent themes in the design are: first, the treatment of interior surfaces in subdued tones and a restricted chromatic range (*above*), and second, the precise framing of exterior views to minimize contrast and emphasize the surrounding greenery (*opposite*).

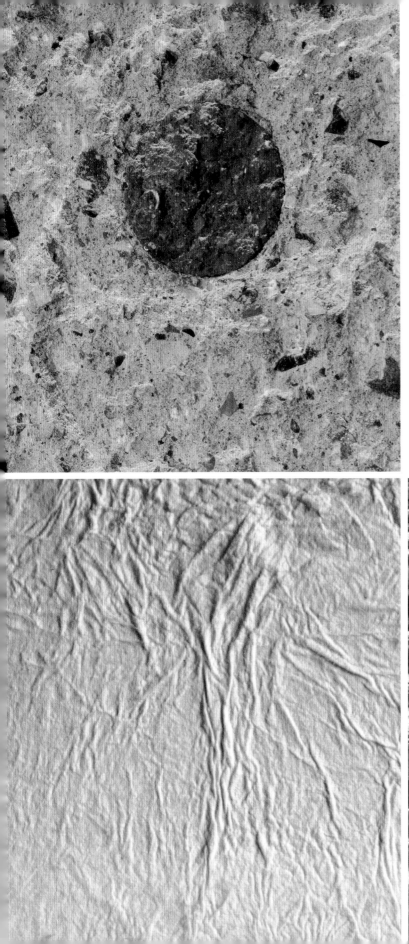

In different parts of the house, Kawaguchi has employed a narrow verticality to add to the sensation of shadow: a triangular space planted with black bamboo adjacent to the entrance is bounded by a high solid wooden fence on one side and concrete wall on the other (*opposite left*); on the other side of the concrete wall (*opposite centre*) a narrow path and steps lead to the double-height main door, while the stairwell (*opposite right*) is of wood painted black, punctuated by pools of light.

Textures also play their part, including a roughly hammered finish to concrete (the same *hatsuri* effect as at the Abode of Clouds house (*p. 162*) *washi* paper laid crinkled on a wall, and plaster that is whisked when first mixed to produce a solidified froth (*this page*).

{Higashi-ya, Tokyo} Shinichiro Ogata is a Tokyo-based designer who chooses to follow through on his work all the way to the end use. In 1998, he started his design company Simplicity 'to create a new type of modern Japanese culture', as he expresses it, and true to this concept has since opened a restaurant and two sweet-shops with a difference. Among the boutiques and cafés of Naka-Meguro, the first sweet-shop, called Higashi-ya, is an odd combination of dilapidated, rusted exterior and minimalist interior. On the ground floor it serves traditional *wagashi* confections to his design, while the upstairs area is a tearoom by day and a bar by night. Ogata's second sweet-shop, called Ori Higashi-ya (the word *ori* implies gift), is in upmarket Nishi-Azabu, at the entrance to Lebain, a combined art gallery, event venue and bath culture store. The atmosphere here accommodates to the white-and-glass modernism of the building, designed by Shigeru Uchida, but has characteristic Ogata touches of eclecticism, including walls of staggered veneer boxes on one side, and paper *origami* panels on the other. Beauty is in the detail, from the newly designed *wagashi* sweets to the packaging. Inside is a counter bar serving food, opening out on to the atrium gallery space of Lebain with its constantly changing shows (flying nylon sheep at the time of photography). This, like the tearoom/bar at the Naka-Meguro branch, also serves as a display area for product design — Ogata has collaborations with a few of Japan's top craft workshops, such as iron foundries in Morioka dating back to the 17th century, white porcelain from Arita and lacquerware from Fukui.

The shop in Nishi-Azabu projects as a glass cube from the all-white office-shop-gallery complex of Lebain (*below*).

Inside, the wall surfaces are a play on the theme of packaging (*right*), which itself is an essential part of the products sold here. On the left, the wall is built of thin wooden boxes laid in courses at irregular depths, and on the right the wall and sliding panel are of folded paper panels.

The sweet counter at the main Naka-Meguro shop (*overleaf*); the wall at left is covered with old wooden moulds for making traditional designs of *wagashi*.

Great care has gone into the design of every detail, from the *origami* paper folding to create panels used on a wall, to the *wagashi* sweets themselves (***these pages***). Bean-paste is widely used for the *wagashi*, which are in a variety of colours, flavours and textures; the black ones contain charcoal, while others are individually wrapped in paper. A water spout fills a white ceramic bowl on the slate counter-top at Nishi-Azabu, and *wagashi* moulds decorate a wall in Naka-Meguro.

The rear of Higashi-ya serves food and drinks at a counter bar, and the surrounding screens can be pulled back to open it to the atrium of the gallery (*left*). In the large central space are regularly changing art exhibits; this installation of flying nylon sheep and oversized black flies is by designers Hideo Mori and Ikuyo Mitsuhashi and titled 'One day, towards the blue sky.'

{Mid-Level Apartment, Hong Kong} Despite the size limitations of this small apartment in Hong Kong's Mid-Levels – its area is only 74 square metres – architect Johnny Li was able to follow some of the most basic principles of Chinese layout and design. The traditional ordering of architectural spaces, argues Li, employs a 'frame system of openings to suggest more space beyond', as can still be seen in, for instance, the scholars' garden dwellings of Suzhou. He achieved the same result in this minuscule space by means of a variety of devices. The prominent wooden frame of the doorway from the small entrance-hall to the living-room stands proud of the wall and is backed by concealed strip-lighting, while one wall of the entrance carries a photographic mural of a moon gate. At the other end of the hallway, a rich purple curtain conceals a small door and implies that the space continues. Windows also receive a framing treatment, and

concealed lighting is used elsewhere to open up the sense of space. Li designed the furniture and fittings, taking old forms, such as hexagons, cloud symbols and opium beds and simplifying their lines for an effect that is modernist with an identifiable Chinese character.

Concealed lighting lifts and enhances the oversized timber frame opening to the vestibule (*right*), where part of the mural photograph of a moon gate can be seen. In a Suzhou Ming garden, a traditional moon gate both frames the view beyond and stresses the continuation of the garden space (*above*).

On the opposite side of the tiny living-room (*below*) from the vestibule (hidden on the right), the corridor leads to bedrooms and bathroom. The curtain at the end suggests more space than there really is. The slatted wooden box conceals the air-conditioning unit.

Concealed lighting at floor level serves both to make one of the bedrooms seem more spacious (*above*), and to make the specially-designed curved bed frame appear to float.

In a second bedroom, two hanging red lampshades are modern, simplified versions of traditional red lanterns, and create a single colour accent in the white space (*opposite*).

{Rachamankha, Chiang Mai} Traditional Thai architecture, at least in its higher forms, draws heavily on religious precedents, notably the design of the buildings of the *wat* — a complex that is part monastery and part place of meditation and worship. The proportions, elements and styles are all very well documented, but until very recently, no serious attempt had been made in Thailand to utilize them intelligently in a modern way.

This is one of the most successful explorations of Thai vernacular — a small hotel complex in the centre of Chiang Mai's old city, designed by its architect-owner Ong-Ard Satrabhandu and completed in 2004. The Rachamankha, just around the corner from Wat Phra Singh, the city's most famous *wat*, combines the simplicity of early Lanna temple architecture with Chinese courtyard layout. Rather than basing his design on the more elaborate city *wat* of Chiang Mai, Chiang Rai, and those of other provincial cities, Satrabhandu found his inspiration in three modest country temples, all on the small scale that once characterized Lanna building. The modern interpretations are evident in the low cloisters around the courtyards, the central pavilion/sitting area in the proportions of an old *viharn*, supported by thick teak pillars, and the sweeping, tiered roof-lines.

The arrangement, naturally, has nothing to do with a monastery, and here the architect drew on the Chinese courtyard house. The ultimate

source of much of the Thai architectural heritage, including the concave flared roofs, is southern China, partly by way of Laos; it seemed appropriate to the architect to import a courtyard layout, although this is not a part of the Thai tradition. The two principal courtyards, lined with cloisters and rooms, are arranged on a north-south axis, joined by an open-sided pavilion which functions as a sitting area for guests. Entrance to the complex, as in a Chinese courtyard house, is from a corner, here via a small corner court to the north-west.

Superimposed flaring roof tiers are characteristic of temple architecture throughout Thailand, but the low proportions here signify a northern heritage (**top** and **right**). The architect chose the purest examples of Lanna religious building as inspiration for the construction. Frangipani trees, like the example here, are favoured in Thailand for their sculptural form. The Viharn Nam Tam (**above**) is the earliest surviving teak religious building in Thailand. This was the model for the central pavilion (**overleaf**).

The structure and proportions of the central, open-sided pavilion (*opposite*) are derived from a 16th-century *viharn*, or assembly hall, at Wat Phrathat Lampang Luang in the next valley to the east of Chiang Mai, and the similarly minuscule *viharn* at nearby Wat Pong Yang Khok.

The design of the low, deeply shaded cloisters that line the two main courtyards (*above*) is taken from those at Wat Thon Kwain, a country monastery to the west of the city.

While the architectural forms derive from Thai temples and palaces of the region – the roof-lines (*left*) largely follow those of the old Governor's house of Lampang – furnishings and objects are principally Chinese. They include statuary, such as a pair of lion-dogs (*opposite below left*) flanking steps, and two stone horses performing the same duty for the restaurant and gallery building (*below*), and furniture, including a Chinese chair in the central pavilion, with a Laotian bronze frog-drum (*below left*). Chinese lattice screens decorate a pavilion at one end of the swimming-pool (*opposite above left*), and two demon faces protect a stone container used as a plant pot (*opposite above right*). It was a Thai dog, however, that stepped into one of the old bricks used as paving (*opposite below right*).

{Art Space N, nr. Yokohama} This two-storey house in a suburb of Tokyo, designed by the architectural team Makoto Shin Watanabe and Yoko Kinoshita of ADH Architects, has an unusual and demanding dual function. Most of the upper floor accommodates the owner's major passion of collecting modern art — a private museum, in fact. It houses an important collection of the German artist Gerhard Richter, as well as works by Marcel Duchamp, the Japanese photographer Hirsoshi Sugimoto and sculptor Kan Yasuda. The aim was to create a series of white spaces under total lighting control — both in terms of quantity and quality.

The specifications for the lighting were exacting. First, the illumination needed to be completely even throughout each of the three gallery rooms. It had to be free of ultra-violet content and at a particular lux value by room. In addition, the colour had to be consistent, whether by day or night, and this meant that natural and artificial light could be mixed in any proportions without colour shifts. The architects' solution was a complex roofing design that admitted daylight but no direct sunlight, yet also incorporated museum-rated fluorescent striplights. The visible light source from within the gallery is the ceiling itself — a taut sheet of 0.5 mm-thick vinyl that acts as the primary diffuser. The mix of lighting falling on this flexible ceiling is regulated by a roof of five parallel aluminium-capped ridges. The V-shaped ducts between these admit indirect daylight through laminated glass sandwiching UV-cutting film. Above and between these skylights are 32W museum colour-corrected fluorescent strips, diffused by vinyl plates. Both daylight and fluorescent sources fall evenly on the vinyl ceiling, and the lamps are on dimmers.

The all-glass façade incorporates light control for the living and study areas, which occupy the front of the house (*right*).

The downstairs gallery at the main entrance (*below* and *overleaf*) houses the owner's collection of contemporary photography, principally German and Japanese.

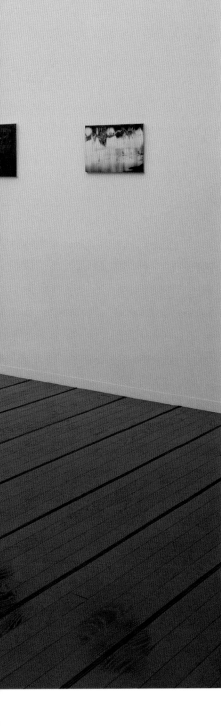

One of the three interconnected galleries on the upper floor (*left*); its dark stained and polished floor and bench set off the white walls and ceiling. The latter is made of tightly stretched translucent vinyl above which there is a mix of colour-balanced fluorescent lamps and baffled daylight. An equal quantity of light thus reaches the entire wall-space.

A small high-walled courtyard at the top of the stairs (*above*) is designed as an exterior gallery; it houses a work in Carrara marble by renowned sculptor Kan Yasuda.

{Nira House, nr. Tokyo} While not exactly a return to nature, this prize-winning house near Tokyo makes a determined effort to integrate house and natural elements in an organic way, and was inspired by the architect's research into old vernacular Japanese forms. In particular, these included the *shibamune*, houses with roofs of living grasses and plants such as lilies, irises, *noshiba* (Zoysia japonica) and *iwahiba* (Selaginella). This ancient roofing method is on the point of extinction, and for Terunobu Fujimori, whose Pine Tree House house appears on p. 196, this is a great loss of an essential part of Japanese culture — the relationship between dwelling and nature. 'What I wanted to do was make plants grow from a building in the way soft downy hair grows out of the skin.'

He created the opportunity with this house for an old friend, the well-known artist and novelist Genpei Akasegawa, whom he persuaded to be involved in the construction. Although a two-storey house with a tall ceiling to the first floor, the steep slope against which it is built puts the roof at street level, and the entrance is across a small drawbridge into the upper floor. This made it practical for Fujimori to make the roof — long and with a shallow pitch — a prominent part of the design. Another plant that was commonly found on *shibamune* is the *nira*, or Chinese chives, best known for the pungent flavour they add to *gyoza* dumplings (U.S. 'pot-stickers') and the architect chose these lowly plants for the roof. Akasegawa was sceptical at first, but Fujimori reassured him that the garlicky smell was only when they were cut. Completed in 1997, the Nira House won the prestigious Japan Art Prize, or Nihon Geijutsu Taisho — significantly as a work of art rather than just a work of architecture.

Arranging for the thousand *nira* to grow healthily on a roof involved considerable experimentation; the solution was found in a concealed watering system, with each plant in a specially designed pot sitting in a tray. All of this required a thousand circular holes to be cut in the roof (**right**).

Because the site covers a steep drop, the entrance is at the upper level and the all-wood building has two floors below this. Seen from below, a wooden passageway bridges the gap at entrance level between the two wings (**below**).

A separate room that projects above the main roof (the box-like structure on the right of the illustration on the previous page) is a highly idiosyncratic tea-ceremony room, with a vaulted roof of ordinary domestic firewood (**above**). This was a communal building effort, by the architect, owner and friends.

The hand-built character is evident throughout. The double-height living-room is finished with rough planking, the uneven joints filled and highlighted with white plaster (**opposite**).

{ARCHITECTS & DESIGNERS}

Architects 49 Limited (A49)
81 Sukhumvit 26 Prakanong Rd.
Bangkok 10110
e-mail: a49@loxinfo.co.th

Makoto Shin Watanabe and Yoko Kinoshita
ADH Architects
3-7-18 Kaigan
Minato-ku
Tokyo 108-0022
website: http://home.att.ne.jp

Studio Giovanni d'Ambrosio,
Via Monserrato, 34
00186 - Rome   ITALY

Shigeru Ban Architects
5-2-4 Matsubara
Setagaya
Tokyo
e-mail:
Tokyo@ShigeruBanArchitects.com

Robert Chan
Nube
58 Tai Cang Lu
Shanghai 200021
e-mail: nube@nubedesign.com

Ian Chee
VX Design & Architecture
Singapore
e-mail: info@vxdesign.com
website: http://www.vxdesign.com

Cheong Yew Kuan
45 Cantonment Road,
Singapore 089748
Tel; 65-67355995
Fax: 65-67388295
e-mail: cykuan@pacific.net.sg

FOBA,
34-3 Tanaka
Todo
Uji-shi
Kyoto 611-0013
e-mail: info@fob-web.co.jp

Terunobu Fujimori
University of Tokyo
Tokyo

**Jean-Michael Gathy,
Denniston Sdn. Bhd**
23rd Floor Plaza Atrium
Lorong P. Ramlee
50250 Kuala Lumpur
Malaysia
e-mail: denniston@denniston.com.my
Tetsuo Goto
4-5-8 Bancho
Takamatsu
Kagawa-ken 760-0017

Yasuhiro Harada
Cube, Inc.
Landic Akasaka Building 8F
2-3-4 Akasaka
Minato-ku
Tokyo 107-0052
website: http://www.cu-be.com

The interior of the Bank of China, Hong Kong, by I.M. Pei (*opposite*).

Ko Shiou Hee
K2LD Architects
136 Bukit Timah Road
Singapore 229838
website: http://www.k2ld.com

Masatoshi Izumi
3720 Mre
Mure-cho
Kitagun
Kagawa-ken
Japan 761-0121

Michimasa Kawaguchi
1-6-1 Koishikawa
Bunkyo-ku
Tokyo 112-0002

Kengo Kuma & Associates
2-24-8, Minamiaoyama,
Minato-ku
Tokyo 107-0062
e-mail: kuma@ba2.so-net.ne.jp
website: www02.so-net.ne.jp/~kuma

Tsutomu Kurokawa
Out.Design Co. Ltd.
2-3-2 Kami-Osaki,
Shinagawa-ku, Tokyo 141-0021
e-mail: info@outdesign.com

Johnny Li
Nail Assemblage International Ltd.
409 Yu Yuet Lai Building
43-55 Wyndham Street
Hong Kong
e-mail: nail@netvigator.com

Yoko Matsumura
1-20-19 Minami Hisagahara
Outa-ku
Tokyo 146-0084
e-mail: yoko@matumura.biz
website: http://www.matumura.biz

Takeshi Nagasaki
N-tree
#406 Inogashira Mansion
1-7-12 Gotenyama
Musashino-shi Tokyo 180-0005
e-mail nagasaki@n-tree.jp
website: http://www.n-tree.jp

Shinichiro Ogata
Simplicity, 1-21-25 Higashiyama,
Meguro-ku, Tokyowebsite:
http://www.simplicity.co.jp

Satoshi Okada Architects
16-12-303 Tomihisa, Shinjuku,
Tokyo 162-0067
e-mail: mail@okada-archi.com
website: http://www.okada-archi.com

P Interior and Associates (PIA)
193/120-121, 29th Floor
Lake Rajada Office Complex
Rachadapisek Road
Klongteoy
Bangkok 10110
e-mail : jad-j@pia-group.com

Ichiro Shiomi and Etsuko Yamamoto,
Spinoff Ltd.
Tokyo
e-mail: contact@spinoff.cc

Studio Myu
1-27-3, Kichijoji-honcho 701
Musashino
Tokyo 180-0004
website: http://www.studio-myu.com

Kohei Sato
3-15-20, Yamanone, Zushi-shi
Kanagawa-ken 249-0002

Ong-Ard Satrabhandu
23 Thonglor 23
Sukhumvit 55
Bangkok 10110

Jun Tamaki
Tamaki Architectural Atelier
2 Higasi Hayaagari Todou
Uji, Kyoto 611-0013
website:
http://wao.or.jp/user/tamaa/maineng.html

Shigeru Uchida
Uchida Design, Inc.
3A, 3-16-28 Nishi-Azabu
Minato-ku
Tokyo 106-0031

Takashi Yamaguchi and Associates
Fusui Building 1-3-4
Ebisunishi, Naniwa-ku
Osaka 556-0003
e-mail: ya@yamaguchi-a.jp
website: www.yamaguchi-a.jp

Ken Yokogawa Architect & Associates
The Terrace, 1-33-1 Makamachidai
Tsuzuki-ku, Yokohama 224-0041
website: http://www.kenyokogawa.co.jp

{Acknowledgments}

In addition to the architects and designers whose cooperation made this book possible, the author would like to thank the following individuals and organizations for their help in its creation:

798 Gallery
Agatha Belinda
Laurence Brahm
Biasa Gallery
Jehanne de Biolley
Melvyn Chua
Cube, Inc.
Thanistha Dansilp
Dynamic Tools Corporation
Neyla Freeman
Fuchun Resort
Judy Gao
Chris and Shigeko Gentry
John and Cynthia Hardy
Maya A. Kishida
Gerald Kong
Krung Thai Bank
Lebain
Ivy Lee
Sharon Leece

Luuk Chang Restaurant
Didier and Marie-Claude Millet
Amon Miyamoto
Miyashita Restaurant
Fumiko Nakato
Rachamankha Hotel
Red Capital Club and Residence
Peter Schoppert and Chor-Lin Lee
Noriko Sakai
Tham Khai Meng
Yoshiaki Toshishige
Tsunami Restaurant
Prabhakorn Vadanyakul
Ambassador Guillermo Velez and
Martha Uribe de Velez
Anne Whetham
Zhan Xin and Pan Shiyi
Sammy Yam, Tian Di Yi Jia Restaurant
Betty Yao
James H. P. Yap

Digital post-production: Yukako Shibata

The central Hong Kong waterfront (*overleaf*).

A digital display looking out over Shibuya Crossing, Tokyo (*page 272*).

STARBUCKS COFFEE